What Entrepreneurs Need to Know

Avoiding Big Mistakes
That Can Prevent Success

By William A. Grimm

Also:
Advice to CEOs and
Outside Board Members

Order this book online at www.trafford.com
or email orders@trafford.com

Most Trafford titles are also available at major online book retailers.

Print information available on the last page.

ISBN: 978-1-4120-7543-5 (sc)
ISBN: 978-1-4251-6707-3 (hc)
ISBN: 978-1-4122-0516-0 (e)

Trafford rev. 05/14/2019

Trafford PUBLISHING www.trafford.com
North America & international
toll-free: 1 888 232 4444 (USA & Canada)
fax: 812 355 4082

Table of Contents

Preface

In speeches and presentations I've given to groups of entrepreneurs, would-be entrepreneurs and advisors to entrepreneurial companies, one of my favorite topics has been mistakes made by development-stage companies. I usually list more than 50 mistakes, each of which can cause serious problems. Whenever I give this talk, members of the audiences shake their heads and laugh as I go through each mistake. Inevitably, several people approach me later to say they've either experienced these mistakes or have observed companies that committed them.

When I started this book, I thought I'd simply go through a long list of mistakes I've observed. As I began writing, I realized the book needed to focus on mistakes that threaten the success of a company. I introduce each chapter with a "war story" I've experienced to illustrate the mistake in the context of a real business situation. I've disguised the name and product of each company involved, but the essence of each story is real. If you recognize the product or service in a war story, you can be sure the story is not about the company you think it is. I've used real products or services in most of the war stories to add context to the message of the chapter. None of the names or products or services in these war stories belongs to the real story behind the message.

The mistakes I address apply to most companies that have raised capital. Since my experience has been primarily with early stage or development-stage companies, most of this book is written from that perspective. However, I've been general counsel to a number of publicly held companies, most of which went public after raising a significant amount of capital from venture capital firms or from experienced angel investors. I believe companies at this level can also benefit from the advice in this book.

My Background

I bring a unique perspective to these observations because of my background. I have a mechanical engineering degree with a concentration in thermodynamics and worked briefly as a sales engineer, then an applications engineer for a major manufacturer of direct current motors and control systems. I served in the U.S. Navy as the supply officer of a destroyer. After the Navy, I obtained an MBA and then worked as assistant to the vice president of marketing for a company that made most of the Apollo space program's ground telemetry stations. These stations were, basically, the early means of wireless digital data communications.

Two engineers from this company started a new company that became known as DataPoint Corporation. I joined DataPoint as its chief financial officer about four weeks after it was founded. Its initial focus was the development of a cathode-ray-tube terminal that could display Teletype information. While this sounds extraordinarily simple today, in 1969 there was no visual display terminal that could show simple Teletype messages. DataPoint went through two rounds of angel financing and an initial public offering.

After DataPoint, I joined a regional investment-banking firm, becoming a vice president of corporate finance. There, I served as a securities analyst as well as an investment banker, raising capital privately and managing several initial public offerings. I was envious of the lawyers who worked on the public offerings because they seemed to be the only people who really knew what they were doing. I decided to cash in my DataPoint stock options, take my family to St. Petersburg, Florida, and attend Stetson University College of Law.

After receiving my law degree, I returned to Orlando, Florida, and started a technology company law practice. I quickly obtained several new companies as clients that had been founded by engineers from the company where I had worked after obtaining my MBA. In short order, I helped several of these companies go through the process of raising capital from venture capital firms. I was able to offer them advice from the viewpoint of a CFO and an investment banker rather than just as a lawyer.

In the early 1980s, as outside general counsel, I helped a laser company go public. Shortly after that, I guided another client through the IPO process as outside general counsel and as a member of its board of directors. The company had gone through two rounds of venture capital financing before going public.

Since that time, I've served as general counsel to many private and public technology companies, most of which had been financed, initially, by angel investors followed by venture capital firms. All venture capital-financed companies are under a great deal of pressure to either go public or be acquired within a certain time frame. Those companies that don't do either usually become part of the living dead – staying alive, but barely. I've also worked with a number of venture capital-financed and angel-financed companies that shut their doors or extended their lives for a short period of time by filing a petition to reorganize under Chapter 11 of the Bankruptcy Act.

About This Book

I haven't written this book in the form of an academic paper or as an article for a law review. I've tried to write this in plain English. This is very hard for a lawyer.

Who can benefit from reading this book? All would-be entrepreneurs as well as current members of the management teams and boards of directors of development-stage companies. When I use the term "development-stage" in this book, I'm speaking of companies from start-up through the stage immediately before going public that have raised or intend to raise at least $1 million by selling equity securities. I often refer to the "products" of the company, but these principles apply equally to companies that offer services. I also frequently refer to company founders and entrepreneurs. These are interchangeable terms.

Most individual investors don't understand what takes place in the boardroom of privately held or publicly held companies. Investors who are tempted to put money into young technology companies can benefit from my observations.

Men and women who are considering joining the management team of a development-stage company or a small-cap publicly held company could benefit from reading this book. It's surprising to me that many CEOs hired to replace founders have never attended a meeting of the board of directors of any company. When they attend their first board meetings, these CEOs are usually shocked by the lack of knowledge about their companies displayed by almost all outside board members. I often "hold the hand" of a new CEO for the first 12 months, coaching him or her on how to work with the board. Although every group is different, the dynamics at work at the board level are the same for almost all boards of directors.

Most development-stage companies have outside directors. I use this term to differentiate these directors from those who are members of the company's management team. Not all outside directors are "independent" as defined by the New York Stock Exchange, the American Stock Exchange, Nasdaq or the Securities and Exchange Commission. Some have relationships with the company that disqualify them from being independent directors.

Sometimes companies insist on having a director who is well-known or even famous, such as a retired general or someone who has held a high-level political position. My observation is that these directors seldom make a contribution to the business of the company since, generally, they know nothing about the actual business of the company – or, often, business in general. However, they can bring high integrity to the board of directors – which, by itself, can be a great contribution to the board.

Outside directors from within the company's industry often bring with them relationships that are valuable, but they seldom make a contribution to the board's strategic decision-making. I've known a number of retired CEOs of technology companies who have become board members of other technology companies. They were extraordinarily dynamic and forceful as CEOs of their own companies but became incredibly passive after joining the new boards. I attribute most of this to not having a significant economic stake in the company and not wanting to cross the CEO, who undoubtedly chose them to serve as board members.

Partners in venture capital firms are very, very smart people. When times are good, they make an incredible amount of money. They perform significant due diligence on a company before making an investment, smoking out all material facts concerning the company and problems that might be lurking, whether the company is aware of them or not. A company that goes through the venture capital financing process is initiated into the financial and business reporting practices it will have to go through someday as a publicly held company.

Every venture capital-financed company I've represented wanted to have an IPO as soon as the stock market would permit. During the dot-com bubble, it was easy for a venture capital-financed company to go public, often as a pure start-up. Those days are over. As the stock market returns to normalcy, the IPO market will rebound, but only for companies with significant revenues that are on a clear success path.

Companies that avoid the mistakes I cover in this book – or, hopefully, recover from them – are more likely than not to be good candidates for IPOs. I hope you take away some of the lessons learned by many real companies that have experienced these mistakes.

1

Not Understanding How Hard it is to Raise Capital

or

"If that company can raise $2 million from venture capital firms, we can easily raise $4 million."

Rob and Ed were working for a large defense contractor when they decided to go into business for themselves. Experts in wireless technology, they had an idea for developing a device called an access point that would allow up to five notebook computers to connect wirelessly to a video projector in a conference room without each presenter plugging wires into the projector. They bought a license from the defense contractor for several patents they needed to develop the device, prepared a business plan, and put $50,000 of their own money into the new company, which they called Epi-Band.

With the help of two part-time engineers, they were able to develop a prototype five months after they started the company. Although neither of the founders had taken a salary up to that point, they had paid the engineers, purchased parts for the prototype, traveled to attend one of the large electronics trade shows, and racked up other expenses. Their $50,000 was gone. They were now using their credit cards, and they knew they had only about two more months before they would reach their limits.

Even so, they were confident they would make it. Before starting Epi-Band, they'd met with a successful entrepreneur who'd left the same defense contractor several months before to form her own company. Rather than develop a new product, though, she started a consulting firm providing engineering services to other defense contractors on a project basis. She started the company with $20,000 of her own money and quickly developed positive cash flow. She kept her overhead low and operated profitably within three months. When she felt she needed to expand, she approached several angel investors and was able to raise $150,000 with little difficulty. She had so little trouble raising capital that Epi-Band's founders believed they'd be able to do it just as easily.

At one of the trade shows they attended, they met a man who introduced himself as an investment banker. After seeing their business plan, he assured them he would be able to raise $2 million from offshore investors in a few weeks. Because he said he had raised capital for several other companies, he asked for a $25,000 front-end payment for business consulting, an option on 15 percent of the stock that would be outstanding after the $2 million investment, and a 10 percent cash commission on the money he raised. He also wanted the exclusive right to raise capital for the company for six months, and to be eligible for the stock and cash commission on any capital raised during the six-month period whether or not he was instrumental in raising it.

Having never been involved in a deal like this before, the two founders sought expert advice and were referred to me.

After hearing their story, I asked to see their business plan and the agreement from the investment banker. I told them I would give the plan a grade of "D+" and that they'd have to bring it up to at least an "A-" if they wanted to raise capital from qualified investors. Needless to say, they were shocked, but they were willing to listen. Walking them through the plan page by page, I pointed out many important omissions, including the shallow treatment they'd given their competition, the market for their product, and the channels through which they expected to sell it. Also, their financial projections grossly understated certain expenses and overvalued the company.

I suggested several ways they could revise the plan. They should consider changing the financial section so that, rather than raising $2 million all at once, they could raise $750,000 initially and $1.25 million nine months later. I told them it would be much more difficult for them to raise capital than it was for their former co-worker because her company, not being involved in product development, had started bringing in revenues from day one. Finally, I told them the chance of the so-called investment banker raising capital for them from offshore investors was almost zero and that they should not sign the agreement. I told them they'd be stupid if they did.

Some weeks later, the founders returned with a new business plan and an interesting – although not surprising – story about their "investment banker." It seems that when, as I had suggested, they'd asked him to allow them to talk to two or three of his previous clients, he told them he couldn't reveal their names because he had to protect the identity of the offshore investors. My guess, of course, is that there were no clients and never had been. The founders wisely decided not to sign his agreement.

They'd also done a good job of revising the business plan. This time I gave it an "A." They were ready to start looking for financing. I explained there are essentially two sources of financing for entrepreneurial companies: venture capital firms and angel investors. I didn't think they were good candidates for venture capital firms because they didn't have revenues yet. Start-up companies typically need to raise at least $1 million from angel investors and generate revenues before they can get the attention of a venture capital firm.

But raising capital from angel investors isn't easy, either. Most angel investors receive several business plans every week and usually don't make more than one or two investments a year. I asked them to imagine an angel investor with 50 business plans on his desk. If this person will invest in only one of these companies, how will he decide? Obviously, the best business plan will be a major factor.

Since, on average, most angel investors will commit only $50,000 initially, if Rob and Ed wanted to raise $750,000 they would have to find 15 investors. Using my rule of thumb of having to contact 10 angel investors for every one who invests, they'd have to approach 150 people, each of whom had the ability to make an investment of at least $50,000.

Not surprisingly, they said they had no idea how they'd find that many potential investors – a problem all entrepreneurs face. I told them to ask every potential investor they spoke with, whether he or she decided to put money into Epi-Band or not, for referrals to one or two other potential investors. Hopefully, by doing so, they'd eventually find a group of angel investors for their company. Fortunately, they took my advice. Even though it took much longer than they expected, they were able to raise the $750,000 they needed to get their wireless access point into production.

Within a few months, they not only had something to sell but also had begun getting orders, at which point they were able to approach several venture capital firms. Eventually, they found one that agreed to act as the lead firm. That firm brought in two others and the three firms invested a total of $3 million into Epi-Band. The company had revenues in excess of $10 million in the third year after the venture capital firms made their investment. Under pressure from the venture capital firms to sell the company so they could recover their investment, the founders sold Epi-Band for about $12 million soon after. Each founder ended up with about $2 million.

Why It's Difficult to Raise Capital

This story had a happy ending, but most stories about start-ups don't. In fact, probably 95 percent of the new companies that try to raise capital from angel investors or venture capital firms don't succeed in doing so. The founders of Epi-Band were unusual. They were quick learners and accepted the advice of their advisors about how hard it is to raise capital. Perhaps even more important, they approached the task of doing so with the same intensity they applied to making their product stand out among its competitors.

Why is it so hard for start-up companies to raise capital? There are several reasons, but the most prevalent is simply that most of them don't represent viable business opportunities. When you start a business, it's usually easy to raise a modest amount of capital from friends and family members because they're irrational investors. They're making an investment because of their relationship with you, not because of the merits of the business. Once you've spent that start-up money and you start looking for serious capital, the situation changes dramatically. Unless your business is sufficiently viable to be of interest to knowledgeable investors, chances are it will either fail after a few years or become one of the living dead. A living dead company is one that's just hanging on and has little hope of growing its revenues or profitability. Often the living dead serve only to provide a modest income to their founders and never provide a way for investors to recover their money.

Even if your company does represent an attractive opportunity for angels or venture capital firms, you have to convince them that of all the opportunities presented to them, yours is the one they should invest in. Imagine this. You have a product you want to sell to the purchasing agent for a large company. You have a meeting and leave him with your sales promotion materials. Unknown to you, though, the purchasing agent has received, or will receive before making his decision, the promotional materials for more than 20 similar products. He doesn't tell you he's considering these other products, nor does he tell you how yours compares. But he makes a decision based on the materials he's received.

Does that sound like a difficult situation? It is. And it's exactly what you face when you start showing your business plan to potential investors.

For that reason, the only way you'll be able to get the financing you're looking for is to make sure your plan provides not just a convincing argument but an *overwhelmingly* convincing argument that your company is a better investment opportunity than any of the others a potential investor might be considering.

Angel Investors

Unfortunately, because of the competition for capital, even having an excellent idea for a business and a dynamite plan is no guarantee you'll be able to find investors. As I told the founders of Epi-Band, there are essentially two potential sources of capital for start-up companies: angel investors and venture capital firms. And it's very difficult to raise money from either, although not necessarily for the same reasons.

Angel investors are typically entrepreneurs themselves who have a net worth of more than $1 million. They believe they can pick winners based on their own success and like to invest in young companies, partly for the potential gain on their investment and partly because of the excitement of being involved in entrepreneurial businesses. As a rule, angel investors invest based on an entrepreneur's business plan and presentation. To a potential investor, a well-prepared business plan shows the entrepreneur's ability to create a strategy and develop an outline for executing it. And indirectly, it shows the entrepreneur's managerial abilities. If the presentation confirms the impression made by the business plan, an entrepreneur has a good chance of getting angels to invest.

It's important to bear in mind, though, that as a rule, angel investors will rarely devote more than 5 percent to 10 percent of their liquid net worth to high-risk investments such as start-up companies. In addition, most angel investors realize that since most of the companies they support will fail, they have to participate in several early stage companies if they hope to make any return on this part of their investment portfolios. What this means in practical terms is that if an angel investor has a liquid net worth of $1 million, he or she will probably be willing to invest $50,000 to $100,000 in one or two early stage companies.

At that rate, if you want to raise $2 million from angel investors, you'll have to find between 20 and 40 who are willing to back your company. And since as a rule you have to talk to 10 potential investors to get one to provide you with capital, you'll have to approach 200 to 400 individuals. For that reason, the greatest difficulty in raising money through angel investors is getting access to enough of them. Few individuals starting their own companies know 200 people with a liquid net worth of $1 million or more.

As I told the founders of Epi-Band, the only way to gain access to a large enough number of potential investors is persistence. You have to ask every potential investor, whether or not he or she invests in your company, to refer you to other potential investors. Hopefully, by doing so, you'll find one who's not only interested in your company but is a member of an investor group and is willing to act as your sponsor. Each group is made up of several angels who unite to invest in companies on a deal-by-deal basis, and there are many of them around the country, particularly in large cities. It's not necessary, though, to find one in your area. These groups are usually willing to invest in promising companies regardless of where they're located.

Unlicensed Brokers

Because it's so difficult to get access to a sufficient number of angel investors, entrepreneurs sometimes become victims of charlatans who offer to raise capital for them. You've probably seen their ads in newspapers or on the Internet. You might even have been approached by one of them. When they hear about a start-up company trying to raise money, they pounce on it, claiming they can bring in large amounts of capital from undisclosed investors, often said to be from South America or the Middle East. Of course, there's a fee for their services, anywhere from $5,000 to $50,000.

Unfortunately, as questionable as these people's claims might be, entrepreneurs are sometimes tempted to use their services. When entrepreneurs give in to that temptation, they invariably wind up losing the up-front fee, not raising capital, and having no remedy against the so-called finder.

As was the case with Epi-Band's founders, when entrepreneurs come to me seeking advice on whether to use a finder like this, I always suggest they ask the finder to provide at least three references from companies that have used his services for raising capital in the past, and to talk to each of those references. Interestingly, in my 30 years of working with start-up companies, I've never had a report from an entrepreneur that the references – if any – ever checked out. I'm sure there must be an exception to this, but if so I've never heard of it.

Moreover, many states prohibit companies from paying fees or commissions in cash, stock or other forms to firms or individuals for raising capital for them unless the firms or individuals are licensed by the state as securities dealers. Because of that, while there are some minor exceptions to this rule, great care must be taken in paying a fee to someone to raise capital for you. The payment of such a fee relating to an investor living in a state where such payments are prohibited will taint the offering. That is, it might cause the entire offering – regardless of where any other investors might live – to violate the securities laws.

Investment Banking Firms

Another potential source of investors that many – in fact, almost all – entrepreneurs approach are investment banking firms such as Merrill Lynch or, more often, smaller local stock brokerage firms. They correctly assume these firms have many clients who are interested in investing in businesses.

Nevertheless, it's almost impossible for entrepreneurs to interest such a firm in finding capital for them for two reasons. First, most of these deals are too small for investment banking firms. Even the small firms are willing to work only on deals of $10 million or more, and large firms are not usually interested unless at least $50 million is involved. Second, such deals carry substantial liability, and even if they're successful, the firm can earn only a small fee at best. There are some small investment bankers that will help exceptional start-up companies raise capital, but there are no such firms in most areas of the country, and those that do exist are very selective. In fact, investment bankers are likely to work with an entrepreneur only in certain situations, such as when the person is starting a third business after having already taken two other companies public.

Stockbrokers

Almost all entrepreneurs I've worked with have also told me they've been approached by stockbrokers who claim they can raise capital for a company. Although this might sound like a tempting offer, accepting it is likely to lead to trouble. The National Association of Securities Dealers, to which all licensed securities dealers must belong, prohibits individual stockbrokers from engaging in this activity unless it's through their firms.

This is, however, an obscure regulation, and many stockbrokers are unaware of it. As a result, when I tell entrepreneurs about this, and they confront the stockbrokers who approached them, the stockbrokers usually claim ignorance. At the same time, though, they apparently have a sense that it might be a problem because they're unwilling to let their supervisors discuss it with the entrepreneurs.

Notices in the Media

I've also had company founders come to me announcing they intend to raise money by making an offering on the Internet, in newspapers, at large meetings of potential investors, or by letters to a mailing list from a magazine such as *Wired*. Although this might seem like a good idea, if you make such an offering the chances are the first person you'll hear from is someone from your state's securities administrator's office or the U.S. Securities and Exchange Commission. That's because it's illegal to make a general solicitation for a private offering of stock.

Why are these kinds of solicitations against the law when they could provide entrepreneurs with access to a large number of potential investors? Because they could also provide unscrupulous individuals with an equally large number of potential victims to defraud. So even though the law might seem like a stumbling block for entrepreneurs, it's there for everyone's protection.

Nevertheless, many entrepreneurs still try to advertise their offerings in these ways. But once an entrepreneur has made a general solicitation, the offering is tainted. In fact, such a situation can be remedied only by returning any money that was raised through these methods, stopping the general solicitations, and waiting at least six months before making the offering again without a general solicitation.

Venture Capitalists

The second of two ways founders of start-up companies can effectively raise funds is from venture capital firms. These firms are typically limited partnerships or limited liability companies with two to five managing partners and $50 million to $200 million to invest. Finding venture capital firms is much easier than finding angel investors. There are more than 500 such firms in the United States, and many directories list their names and addresses, the names of their partners, and their areas of interest. Several of these directories are listed in the Appendix in the back of this book.

The real challenge with such firms is getting them to read your business plan and take a serious interest in your company. Most venture capital firms don't invest in start-ups, and those that do are incredibly selective. These firms receive hundreds of business plans every year, so simply sending out copies to a list of firms isn't likely to achieve your goal. The only practical way to get such a firm interested is to be referred by someone who already has credibility with the partners. Perhaps not surprisingly, the best sources for such referrals are successful entrepreneurs who have raised capital from several of the venture capital firms. However, these firms also will seriously consider referrals from experienced venture capital lawyers, accounting firms, and, on occasion, investment bankers. It's important to remember that all such a referral can guarantee is a cursory reading of your plan. After that, your plan must stand on its own merits.

Although getting a referral to a venture capital firm can be even more difficult than finding a sufficient number of angel investors, if you can get a referral there are several benefits to working with such firms. One of the most important is that each has a network of other venture capital and investment banking firms. These organizations also often have relationships with potential large customers and suppliers, and they have sources of business intelligence – including those with information about your competition – that can't be obtained otherwise. In addition, they will bring discipline to your board and make the group function as directors instead of giving a rubber stamp to the founders.

Raising money from venture capital firms is much too complex a subject to be discussed adequately here. I've included in the Appendix a list of several excellent books on the subject and would strongly urge you to read several of them before trying to raise capital from such firms.

Understanding What Creates Value for Investors

Founders seldom know what creates value in the eyes of venture capital investors or other investors during the development stage of a company. If the founders have any knowledge of value creation, it's usually superficial – and naturally, they don't realize that.

What is it that causes a step-up in valuation for a company as it goes down the path of raising different layers of capital? What does it mean to have "up rounds" of financing in order to establish the momentum of valuation? How do you live with "down rounds"?

Things are different for entrepreneurs since the financial bubble burst in the early 2000s. Today, instead of raising $20 million for its first round of venture financing, usually referred to as the "Series A" round, a development-stage company is likely to raise less than $5 million at this point. In fact, that first round of financing is now more likely to come from angel investors instead of venture capital firms. A new technology company will now have to raise $1 million to $2 million from angel investors before the company makes enough progress to appeal to venture capital firms. Of course, there are exceptions to this, such as when the company founders have extraordinary experience, or when the technology that forms the basis for the company is coming from a large organization that invested heavily in it. Otherwise, a development-stage company must approach angel investors first.

After raising capital from angel investors, the company may raise $5 million to $7 million from venture capital investors in the "B" round of funding, and it probably will need another round of venture financing before it's a candidate for an initial public offering.

Since almost all company founders have no experience in raising venture capital, they seldom know the milestones that must be met in order to make the company attractive to venture capital firms. It only follows that they don't have these milestones in their business plans when they raise capital from angel investors as the first step toward raising venture capital.

Most angel investors are much less demanding on start-up companies than venture capital investors, which require companies to have well-defined strategic objectives and milestones. Yet many start-ups that have raised $1 million to $2 million from angel investors believe they can raise the next round from venture capital firms merely by having letters of intent or some type of positive testimonials from knowledgeable people in their industry supporting their claims for their products. I always advise these companies to find some way to have a customer pay money for the company's product or service as a critical milestone before approaching venture capital firms.

All venture capital firms know it's simply too easy to get letters of intent or some type of testimonials from engineering managers of potential customers who say they love the company's technology and products. Only when a customer pays money for the company's product is a testimonial from that customer valuable. If a start-up company can't establish some type of traction with customers within the capital provided by angel investors, it's highly unlikely venture capital firms will want to get involved.

Each development-stage company is different and will need to meet its own set of milestones to create shareholder value. However, all of the milestones are related. They're major accomplishments that will lead to customer traction. They might include completing a product prototype and showing it at the annual industry trade show; producing 10 pre-production versions of the product; placing three units with customers at company expense to obtain accurate feedback on their performance; obtaining a report by an industry expert favorably comparing the company's product to those of competitors; or presenting a paper at one or more conferences highlighting the company's product.

Venture capital firms that participate in the first round of venture funding will tell the company in no uncertain terms what milestones must be met before the company can secure a second round. These milestones will still be aimed at increasing customer traction, but in a larger way.

Most founders think company valuation is determined by what price per share investors are willing to pay at any given time for shares of stock in the company. For example, if an angel investor is willing to pay $1 per share for 100,000 shares of common stock, which equals 1 percent of the outstanding shares of the company, founders will tell me their company has a value of $10 million. They're usually upset with me when I tell them a purchase of 1 percent of the stock doesn't establish the company's valuation. A purchase of 20 percent of the stock would be good evidence.

Too often, an angel investor will be naïve enough to buy 1 percent of a company for $100,000 when the company should be valued at $2 million at the most. When this happens, the company has already erected a barrier to raising additional capital. The company's valuation expectation is far too high and the founders hate the thought of telling the angel investor that other investors are not willing to pay the price he or she paid.

If venture capital firms are interested, it's likely the proposed valuation for their investment will relate primarily to the milestones achieved and not to the price per share paid by angel investors. Having achieved these milestones demonstrates that the company can execute its strategy. Knowing what milestones must be achieved and achieving them is what creates shareholder value.

Advice for Raising Capital

As an entrepreneur, you have to face the reality that raising capital is hard. Find a way to deal with it. If you can't, it might be better for you to not start a company at all than to start one only to fail and see your investment – as well as money from your family and friends – disappear because you can't find the additional funding you need to continue.

If you do choose to pursue it, I have three pieces of advice:

First, read every book available on the subject of raising capital. Some of those I consider to be among the best are listed in the **Appendix**. There's a great deal of experience reflected in these books.

Second, rely heavily on your advisors during this process: your attorney, your accountant, and the experienced business executives you have, hopefully, asked to serve on your board. These people can provide you with invaluable advice on raising capital.

Finally, speak with successful entrepreneurs who have raised capital from either angel investors or venture capital firms. Their advice will provide the most valuable insight you can get.

2

Failing to Understand the Market and the Competition

or

"How were we supposed to know Sony was developing a handheld computer that was better than ours?"

Dan and Bill started DanCo, an Internet company built around a unique database program originally developed for analyzing stock price movements. They designed a system that would keep track of scores and other performance results of amateur sporting events ranging from Pop Warner Football, Little League and high school soccer to men's tennis leagues and bowling. The database program made it easy for sports fans to keep track of information and for players and coaches to enter data as well, after paying a membership fee.

Dan and Bill believed sporting goods companies would advertise on this Web site, producing significant revenues for the company. They raised more than $1 million from angel investors and launched the company. In preparation, they did not interview a single decision maker at a major sporting goods company to test the assumption that these organizations would flock to the Web site to advertise their products. Instead, they relied on the opinion of a retired sports figure who told them there was a significant market for this advertising.

They found, much to their dismay, that their anticipated advertiser base would not consider spending precious advertising dollars until DanCo had more than 100,000 members entering data on the site. They also discovered that major amateur sports organizations, such as Little League and Pop Warner football, would not allow their teams to use the system unless DanCo paid them a fee. Further, they learned several of the amateur sports organizations were developing their own Web sites to perform a similar function. Unlike DanCo, each of these would be dedicated to a particular sport and attract a core group of enthusiasts.

Dan and Bill developed an outstanding product that performed well and was easy to use. Yet they couldn't get close to achieving the 100,000-member level required by sporting goods companies before they ran out of money.

Despite desperate efforts to sell DanCo, the company closed its doors and the investors suffered a complete loss. The reason: Dan and Bill failed to thoroughly study the market and analyze the potential competition before launching their company. For about $10,000, they could have traveled to five or six sporting goods companies and spent just 15 minutes with the chief marketing officer of each, where they would have learned they'd need to meet a membership requirement before attracting the interest of potential advertisers. Further, if they had simply contacted several of the amateur sports organizations, they would have discovered there was competition on the horizon as these groups planned their own similar Web sites and they could have determined how DanCo could corner its share of the market.

Understanding Market Intelligence

To focus on satisfying real customers demands, companies must have accurate and timely market intelligence, or an understanding of all the major forces that could affect demand for the company's products or services. Companies too often fail because they're blindsided by major economic and competitive forces only to learn, too late, that they're not positioned in the marketplace to succeed. Their products or services no longer meet, or perhaps never have met, the needs of the target customers. Most development-stage companies suffer from this lack of market intelligence right from the beginning.

I know this concept of market intelligence must seem obvious. However, most management teams spend 80 percent of their time on activities such as developing human relations plans or programs, designing incentive compensation packages, dealing with supplier issues, and preparing and revising budgets to a level of accuracy that is unrealistic because the documents are outdated one day after they've been prepared. These executives spend only 20 percent of their time, if that, gathering and analyzing information about competition, market trends, economic and technological forces, and the like. Is it any wonder their companies are blindsided?

In any organization, at least one senior executive officer should spend 80 percent of his or her time on strategy and strategic matters, including gathering and understanding market information. In development-stage companies, this should be the chief executive officer.

Reasons Businesses Fail

Many CEOs blame business failures on lenders pulling the plug on funding, or on the loss of major customer contracts, or on development of foreign competition. In every one of these failures, the root cause is the company's lack of information about the environment in which it's operating. This is true for large and small companies.

If we look with hindsight at any significant business demise, we can see it was caused by the company's failure to understand the market it served. Sometimes this happens because the market is declining and the company is unable to respond by going into new markets. In other cases, competitors drive the company out of its target market. In some instances, companies find they've been chasing a market that doesn't exist.

None of the spectacular business failures we've seen recently occurred because the company was overpaying its mid-level managers, or because it didn't have a dynamite incentive plan, or it failed to implement a quality management program, or it failed to offer competitive benefits to employees. These companies failed because of inadequate market intelligence.

Some of the most prominent recent failures occurred because the companies acquired other organizations without understanding the economic forces and competitive dynamics affecting them. These companies were following an opportunistic strategy driven by the short-term effects of these acquisitions on earnings rather than a well-thought-out plan dictated by major economic and competitive forces.

Gathering Market Intelligence

I've always been amazed at the unwillingness of management teams to devote significant resources to market intelligence, which I define as knowing what customers and competitors are doing, knowing which technological and economic forces are developing, and understanding which major threats the company could face.

Many companies will start out with a so-called SWOT analysis, which examines strengths, weaknesses, opportunities and threats. However, this is usually done at such a superficial level that it's almost worthless. Most executives simply don't have experience at analyzing all of these forces or in gathering information about them. Instead, they rely on anecdotal evidence based on their own experience or information gathered from salespeople who, in turn, gather information from their customers' rank-and-file employees.

Instead, CEOs should spend a large part of their time with customers to get a better sense of the marketplace and competition. CEOs should read various heavy-duty publications about the economic and technology environment. Simply reading the *Wall Street Journal* every day does not meet this requirement.

Large companies try to gather market intelligence by engaging well-known consultants and by obtaining analyses of major economic forces from organizations such as The Conference Board. Small companies can't afford to do this. For these organizations, the CEO's skills in gathering market intelligence become even more critical.

The Board's Role

A board of directors can head off failure by frequently reviewing the company's fundamental strategy, which includes analyzing the organization's market intelligence. Qualified directors can tell whether members of the management team have done their homework.

If several members of the board are willing to ask difficult questions and are unable to get good answers, the management team will be under significant pressure to get its act together. This way the board of directors can make sure the management team understands all the competitive, technological, economic and other forces that affect the company strategically.

3

Not Understanding the Difference Between Customer Need and Customer Demand

or

"Our customers have to be educated about why they need our product."

Edwin and Bill started a company to develop a new antenna that could be used for cellular communications. They had ideas about antenna design that could improve the signal strength emitted by a cellular antenna by a factor of 10. They knew the development effort would take more than $1 million but decided to raise $500,000 initially, intending to raise another $500,000 after they had made progress on the design. By doing this, they believed they could sell fewer shares of stock overall than if they tried to raise $1 million at the beginning.

Their business plan had several technical milestones to be met with the $500,000. When they presented this business plan, they discovered that angel investors also wanted a milestone relating to expressions of customer interest. However, Edwin and Bill didn't feel they needed that milestone at this point because they'd probably be seeking the second $500,000 before the product development would be far enough along for them to show the new antenna to potential customers. They were able to raise the first $500,000 based on the business plan they had prepared.

They made progress in developing a prototype of the antenna. They were close to running out of the initial $500,000 and began to seek investors for another $500,000. At each investor presentation, they were criticized for not having testimonials from potential customers about the benefits of the new antenna. They hurriedly tried to make presentations to several potential customers but found it would take several weeks to get in front of anyone who would have the authority to give such a testimonial. Further, they discovered they had to convince the engineers in each of the potential customer organizations of the merits of the antenna before they could get to the decision-makers.

They had based their belief there was a market for the new antennas on their own analysis, not on any reliable input from bona fide customers. When they had a hard time convincing rank-and-file engineers that their antenna design would improve the performance of the cell phone, they should have gotten the message there was no demand for this improvement. Further, when they finally did get to talk to a vice president at one of the potential customer companies, they learned the customer would never commit to their antenna because of previous bad experiences dealing with small companies.

After about three years, several of these companies did become interested in the antenna and seek out the company. Unfortunately, the company had run out of cash and closed its doors about a year earlier. Edwin and Bill had confused need with demand. They perceived a customer need for this product, but young companies can't survive on perceived needs. There has to be actual demand for their products. Demand is when a potential customer says, "I will buy the product you're offering from either you or another supplier. Tell me why your product is better and I'll give you the order."

The Difference Between Need and Demand

I've been amazed for more than 30 years that chief executive officers, chief financial officers and many members of boards of directors don't understand the difference between need, as perceived by the company, and demand for a product or service. This is especially true of development-stage companies trying to introduce a new product or service. Most often, these companies have been started by engineers and not by marketing people. I'm afraid this is another case of "you don't know what you don't know."

People who have not studied marketing, as opposed to sales, often don't recognize the difference between need and demand for a product or service. They think need equals demand. I try to tell these people there is a supply-demand curve as a function of price, but there's a good reason you don't see supply-need curves.

A symptom of this misunderstanding is the CEO telling potential investors that "this is an education sell to customers, but when they understand the advantages of the product, they will buy the product." In other words, the CEO believes there's a need for the product in the marketplace and potential customers often confirm this by giving glowing statements about the need this product will fulfill. However, it takes forces, economic or technological, to convert need to demand across a large section of potential customers. No small company, let alone a large company introducing a new product, should ever attempt to create the force needed to convert need to demand.

Another way of stating this is the old saying that "pioneers in a marketplace get killed." This is an expression often used by engineers but not really understood. In other words, a "pioneer" in a marketplace is usually trying to convert need to demand through a selling effort that's incredibly expensive, and the response from potential customers is usually low. The follow-up to the expression that pioneers get killed is that the followers of the pioneers often succeed.

Let Large Companies Educate the Market

A successful strategy often followed by development-stage companies is to allow large companies to "educate the market" for a particular product and then come in behind the large companies to provide a product that's targeted at a niche within the market. This is, in essence, a follower strategy. Of course, if the niche market doesn't grow significantly, the development-stage company won't, either.

It would be a mistake for most small companies to enter a niche market not served by the large companies and expect to eventually expand into and become a competitor across-the-board with them. Yet many entrepreneurs think this is a viable strategy. They think they can penetrate the larger market by underpricing the larger companies.

Any small company that thinks it can take business away from larger companies on a sustainable basis by underpricing identical or similar products is in for a rude awakening. For that strategy to work, the company offering the lowest price had better be producing the product at the lowest cost. Otherwise, companies that have large profit margins in the product can easily reduce their prices to match those offered by the small company and drive the small company out of business. Whenever I hear a young company saying its primary strategy will be to offer its product at a significantly lower price than the major competitors, I know this company has been founded by people who don't have strategic business sense.

Making Revenue Projections

Another way of looking at the "need versus demand" problem is that there's an adoption period in any given marketplace for any new product. In technology, companies refer to early adopters as the types of customers who want to be on the leading edge and are willing to take risks by buying products from development-stage companies that have new or improved products.

The unknown factor, and the primary source of risk with a company like this, is the variable length of the adoption period. Young companies usually build into their revenue projections a slowly increasing revenue curve, followed at some point in the future by a rapidly increasing revenue curve. This is called the "hockey stick revenue curve." If a young company doesn't have this in its revenue projections, it'll have a difficult time raising capital.

The inflexion point where the slow growth in revenues turns into a high growth rate is where the company is predicting the beginning of widespread adoption of the product. All venture capital investors know this is almost always a 100 percent guess by the young company. On the other hand, angel investors tend to believe the projections made by young companies, thinking the founders know with a high degree of confidence when they will see widespread adoption of the company's product. Angel investors suffer from the "you don't know what you don't know" syndrome – but, of course, they don't know they suffer from it.

Most angel investors make a few telephone calls to friends in the industry that is the target market for the company's product and hear, anecdotally, the same thing the company is hearing about the need for this kind of product. The angel investors are impressed and don't take time to further examine when this need will convert into demand. In other words, the angel investors make the same mistake the company does in trying to predict when significant revenues will occur.

Development-stage companies that introduce a new product into a market where there is no obvious competition face this problem. Whenever entrepreneurs tell me there's a tremendous need for their product and no clear competition, I see a major red flag. There's no clear competition because the need has not yet turned into demand. The founders face a huge risk that the demand won't occur before the company runs out of money.

4

Making Unnecessary Long-term Commitments

or

"We got a really good deal on our office space by signing a 10-year lease."

Colonel Lewis, newly retired as the commanding officer of a major Air Force hospital, decided to start a company to provide blood analysis services to hospitals, clinics and doctors. Because of his background, he was able to raise $800,000 in equity capital from local investors, mainly doctors, and arranged to lease an expensive computerized blood analysis system. He also leased two-thirds of a floor in an otherwise empty two-story office building.

Shortly after the colonel moved in, the landlord approached him with an offer to sell the building to his company. By buying the building and leasing out the remaining space, the landlord explained, the company could lower its net monthly payments for its own offices by 50 percent. The colonel liked the idea. He told his board members he'd be able to buy the building for $2 million, put down only $400,000 in cash, and get a $1.6 million mortgage. They enthusiastically approved the purchase.

By the end of 18 months, though, the company still hadn't been able to lease the other space in the building. Instead of the company's monthly payments being 50 percent lower than the initial lease payments, they were substantially higher. The company still wasn't breaking even, and because it had used $400,000 of its capital to buy the building, it had exhausted its cash. Without cash, the company had to close its doors, and the colonel had to file for personal bankruptcy because he'd personally guaranteed both the lease on the equipment and the mortgage on the building. And, of course, the investors lost all of their money.

Colonel Lewis made the same mistake as many other entrepreneurs.

He made an unnecessary long-term commitment, in this case using equity capital to make a capital investment, and left his company with too little cash as a reserve against the risk that it wouldn't achieve break-even when expected. If the colonel had been aware of the danger of making such a commitment during the start-up phase, or had enlisted an experienced businessperson on his board who could have warned him and the other board members about it, his company probably would have survived.

Drawbacks of Long-term Agreements

All young companies try to get the best deal, such as the lowest price per unit or the lowest price per square foot, when they're arranging to buy or lease things or to use services. They're often willing to make long-term commitments to get these prices.

Too often, the company founder is in for a serious wake-up call when he or she decides the company can no longer afford to purchase or perform under a long-term agreement. The founder simply decides to stop performing under the agreement and to complain that his or her company should be allowed to cancel the agreement. The founder does not realize the agreement can be enforced and the consequences can be devastating.

I find this to be most troubling when a young company, trying to get the lowest per-unit price on a particular component in a system it intends to make, enters into an agreement calling for the purchase of a large number of these items over the next 12 months. The seller of these items offers a significantly lower per-unit price if the company will commit to buy a large quantity. As the year progresses, the company realizes it cannot possibly use all the items it contracted to buy and notifies the seller it wants to either terminate the agreement or reduce the quantity covered by the agreement. Or the development-stage company commits to purchase thousands of units when it is foreseeable the company will need only hundreds. The company simply thinks it can take delivery for its actual needs, never be required to buy the remaining units, and still receive the per-unit price for the large purchase quantity.

Unless there's a provision in the agreement that allows the company to back out of part of the deal, the company is bound to purchase all the items. If the company does not, the seller is entitled to recover damages in a lawsuit for at least the profit the seller would have made had the items been purchased. Founders of development-stage companies are usually shocked when advised by their lawyers that the seller will win the lawsuit.

Sometimes there are bill-back terms that allow the seller to increase the price on a retroactive basis if the buyer doesn't purchase all the items on the order. This is usually a good provision for the development-stage company, giving it an escape valve. Of course, the company needs to be prepared to pay the retroactive price.

Understanding the Contract

Many company founders worked in larger companies where they had little to do with the purchasing function and simply observed that, whenever the company wanted to cancel a contract or reduce the quantity under contract, the seller simply agreed. What the company founder didn't know is the contract had a provision allowing this or that some consideration was paid to the seller to accomplish this result. Instead, the company founder thinks a simple notification to the seller accomplished the termination of the agreement or a reduction in the number of items to be purchased.

As usual, this is another case of "you don't know what you don't know." Most company founders don't know of the existence of the Uniform Commercial Code that almost every state has adopted governing the terms of the purchase and sale of goods. The UCC supplies missing terms in an agreement for the purchase and sale of goods when these terms are not contained in a written agreement between the parties.

I often see young companies making large purchase commitments using a purchase-order form showing only the price, the quantity and the delivery dates. That is, there are no other terms on the reverse side of the purchase order, as anyone with experience in purchasing would expect. The seller often simply acknowledges the purchase order by sending back a signed copy of it to show acknowledgement of the order.

If this is the case, the UCC takes over and provides almost all the terms of the order. On the other hand, if the seller is a large company that undoubtedly knows about the UCC and the "battle of the forms," the seller will acknowledge the purchase order with an acknowledgement form that has a full back page of terms governing the sale of the goods. The buyer doesn't realize the terms are now governed by the terms set forth on the seller's acknowledgement form. Ninety-nine percent of the time, everything goes as planned in these situations. But when difficulty arises, founders are surprised to find the terms on the back of the acknowledgement form are not favorable to the development-stage company. Duh!

In other instances, young companies issue purchase orders on forms that do have terms printed on the reverse side, but those terms make no sense in the context of the company's business. The company has simply copied someone else's purchase-order form without even reading the terms the company is using for the purchase of goods and services. This shows the lack of attention development-stage companies pay to purchasing or to contract matters in general.

Getting Expert Advice

It's not necessary for development-stage companies to engage a lawyer for every transaction. In fact, even for large commitments, the development-stage company could engage a purchasing consultant, someone who has significant experience in purchasing and contract writing, rather than using the company's lawyer. Not only is this likely to be more cost-effective, the development-stage company founder will usually trust the advice given by a consultant for these kinds of things more than the advice of a lawyer. That's because most lawyers for development-stage companies have little business experience in general and even less knowledge of the development-stage company's specific business. Therefore, the lawyer's advice is seldom given in the context of the company's business.

Company founders realize this quickly and know there's a learning curve for the lawyer even in mundane things such as purchase orders and purchase commitments. It's usually easier for founders to find a consultant with experience in the company's business.

Of course, there are times when companies make large commitments that simply are not governed by the standard terms and conditions found on the reverse of the purchase order. In those cases, the company should engage the services of a lawyer who can explain all the risks and obligations.

Leasing Office Space

Another instance where I find development-stage companies over-committing themselves is in leasing office or manufacturing space. It's almost certain development-stage companies will commit themselves to leasing more office or manufacturing space than they need at the time with the view that they'll need the added space soon based on their growth projections. The company will sign a lease for five years rather than one. Once again, the company founders focus on the price per square foot and realize a one-year lease will carry a higher price than a five-year agreement. Because company founders are always optimistic, they don't view signing a five-year lease as a risk.

And because they don't view it as a risk, they don't have the lease reviewed by a lawyer. More than half of my development-stage clients over the years have signed multiple-year leases with landlords who said these were standard leases. When you're looking at commercial space, there is no such thing as a standard-form lease. Many of the terms are negotiable.

As is often the case, a development-stage business does not develop as rapidly as it predicted or, in fact, has a downturn. Suddenly the company is faced with leasing more space than it can use. If the company has not had the lease reviewed by a real estate lawyer or another competent real estate person, the lease is not likely to permit subleasing or early termination. The lease also might contain burdensome terms to cover the situation if the lessee defaults. Further, in most states, the landlord has a lien on all the tangible property located in the leased facilities to secure the payment of rent. Development-stage company founders seldom know all of this and think they can simply move out of the space or reduce their operation into a smaller portion of the space and the landlord will rent the excess to someone else.

Inevitably, the company is surprised when the landlord sues the company and gets a judgment for the entire sum of the remaining lease payments. Although the law in most states requires the landlord to use its reasonable efforts to lease the space to others if the company defaults on the lease, this duty can be modified or eliminated by the terms of the lease. Company founders often don't even read the lease terms until they find themselves in default or about to default under the lease. They view the lease as simply "boilerplate."

Sometimes It's OK to Pay More

Really smart company founders try to rent space on a month-to-month basis, realizing there's a risk the landlord will find another tenant and give the development-stage company 30 days' notice to leave. However, in my entire experience as a lawyer, I have never seen this happen since landlords are usually happy to have the space rented. Of course, renting space on a month-to-month basis will require a much higher rent per square foot than a five-year lease for the same property. The higher rent per square foot is essentially a price paid to have flexibility if things don't go as predicted.

One reason development-stage companies will often sign long-term leases is to assure them of having contiguous office or manufacturing space as they grow. The reasoning behind this usually is the company can operate more efficiently under a single roof. I know there are some efficiencies if all the employees can be in the same building or at least in a cluster of buildings next to one another. However, this efficiency pales in comparison to the risk a development-stage company takes if it over-commits for space that it later finds can't be used.

Some of the most successful companies I've worked with rented or leased only the space they needed and used that space until it was almost unbearable with crowding before getting other space that was within 10 or 15 minutes' travel time from the original building. Employees cope with this and the whole system can be adapted to allow for the inconvenience of having multiple facilities located in places where a short drive is required.

Smart investors will always be impressed when a company knows how to hedge against risks that are within the company's control. Even though a company might be able to get a lower price per unit by making a long-term commitment, the more important thing is to preserve capital for the time when the company faces an unexpected slowdown. One method of preserving capital is to avoid long-term commitments that can quickly turn into unwanted liabilities.

5

Not Realizing Contracts Are Enforceable

or

"We ordered 10,000 special transceivers at $120 each to get a 30 percent lower price per part, but I know we can get out of the contract if we don't need that many."

Several years ago, I served as general counsel and a member of the board of directors of a software company in Tampa. The company was founded by two people with experience in programming IBM computers to perform data acquisition on various processes, including those in the petrochemical, paper manufacturing and electric generation fields. The company worked with engineering firms that obtained contracts from major companies in these industries. Each engineering firm would be the prime contractor to develop a large-scale data acquisition system and would subcontract with this company to provide the customized software. The projects were large enough to require IBM mainframe computers.

Over several years, the company began developing standard software modules it could use as building blocks for each project. This allowed the company to reduce the price of its services and to significantly improve the schedule for developing customized software for each project. Because the company was entering into sizable business deals, it hired a contract manager from a large local defense contractor. This person was not a lawyer but had a great deal of experience in preparing and revising contracts of this type.

The company found the fastest-growing market for its services was in fossil fuel and nuclear power plants, so it began focusing its efforts on the nuclear power industry.

Until this time, the company had designed and developed the data acquisition software, and the engineering firm that served as the prime contractor handled the systems integration work. That meant the engineering firm was responsible for identifying and buying the required computers, specifying the functions the software would perform, integrating the software with the hardware, installing the software, and training the customer's employees to operate the system.

After the software company had done work for a large electric utility in the Northeast, the utility approached the company to serve as the systems integrator rather than contracting with an engineering firm that would then subcontract with the company. The company had little experience in systems integration but found this opportunity too good to pass up.

The CEO had kept the board of directors advised about this large opportunity. However, the board didn't realize the company was being asked to serve as systems integrator. The board believed the electric utility company itself would handle systems integration and the company would only provide the software for the project. The board was assured the company would not be required to buy the IBM mainframe computers and install them.

Because of the nature and size of the nuclear electric generation plant under design, two complete computer systems would be used to monitor plant operations. One would be on-site and the other several miles away. Both systems would operate in parallel so that if one failed, the other was already in operation.

The company submitted a comprehensive proposal and was awarded the contract, its largest ever and the only one not received through an engineering firm. The company's contract manager negotiated the deal. The company's proposal contained an analysis leading to the conclusion that a certain size of IBM mainframe was required for each computer site to operate the software. The proposal clearly stated the electric utility would buy these computers directly from IBM. The contract manager and the engineering team that wrote the proposal believed the document clearly specified the power company was responsible for determining the proper size of the IBM computers and that the calculations in the proposal were in the form of an example.

When the contract was drafted by the electric utility, the language was ambiguous about the responsibility for determining the size of the IBM mainframes that would be required. In reviewing the draft from the utility, the company's contract manager did not view the proposed language as inconsistent with the company's proposal. He offered many comments about other elements of the agreement but didn't propose any changes in the wording about the size of the mainframes. The contract contained a customary provision that stated the contract superseded all prior negotiations and discussions, including any proposals.

At the time, the company's annual revenues were about $15 million. This single contract was worth about $20 million over three years, or almost $7 million annually. It was the company's largest single contract ever.

The contract manager had not run this contract by me or by another lawyer in my firm who helped the company on routine matters. He felt confident this was a contract in the ordinary course of business for the company. He also believed, from observing contract disputes while he was with his previous employer, that lawsuits over these matters were rare.

Nine months later, the company's software engineers concluded the size of the computers the electric utility had ordered from IBM for the project for $9 million were grossly inadequate to handle the software that would perform the functions specified. The utility had used the sizes the company suggested in its initial proposal, which the company had given as an example only. The company advised the electric utility the computers it had purchased would be inadequate to do the job. The computers the company needed actually would cost about $15 million.

The electric utility was very upset. In addition to already purchasing the computers, the utility had already done extensive site preparation for the computers. For larger computers to be installed, that work would have to be redone. Further, the electric utility would have to order the new computers, which would have a delivery time of almost one year, delaying completion of the project by at least six months.

The company received a letter from the electric utility demanding that the company take responsibility for this error, take all actions necessary to replace the computers, and take responsibility for all of the site preparation expenses that would be incurred because of the error. The company's contract manager called me that day.

When I looked at the contract, I immediately realized any judge interpreting it would side with the electric utility about the company's responsibility for specifying the size of the computers. I did not have all the background about the proposal and had not been present with the contract manager during internal discussions at the company. From an objective legal standpoint, I did not view the contract as ambiguous at all. And it was not in favor of the company.

The CEO and I advised the board of directors of this problem the next day and decided we'd have to issue a press release summarizing the claim made by the electric utility. We, of course, knew this would be devastating to the price of the stock, but the press release was necessary.

I launched an intensive investigation into all the correspondence between the electric utility and the company both before and after the two had entered into this agreement to see whether there were any documents that might support the company's position that the utility was responsible for determining the size of the computers. Unfortunately, I discovered correspondence from a low-ranking engineer at the electric utility to a low-ranking software engineer in the company making it clear the utility expected the company to be responsible for the sizing of the computers. The software engineer had responded that he understood and agreed. Although he did not have the authority to make this agreement, this correspondence would be devastating to the company's position.

The company was working on a progress payment basis with the electric utility and at that time was owed more than $5 million for work already performed. The company estimated it had to perform an additional $5 million of work to complete the software and systems integration.

The company's contract manager organized a conference with the most senior executive involved in this project for the electric utility, the electric utility's counsel, the CEO of the company and me in Washington, D.C., a neutral city. The purpose of the meeting was for the company to make a case that it was not responsible for the computer-sizing mistake that had occurred, although the electric utility didn't know this was our purpose.

We met in Washington and the contract manager and I used every argument we could muster in good faith. As could be predicted, this did not impress the electric utility's counsel. The entire dispute was over the meaning of one sentence in the contract.

One of the responsibilities of a lawyer in reviewing contracts of this type is to eliminate or minimize the risk of something going wrong for the lawyer's client. It was clear that any lawyer, even one six months out of law school, could have written a sentence or paragraph that would have made it clear the company had no responsibility for sizing the computers and that the size previously discussed was for example only and not binding on the company. This would have jumped out as a giant red flag to any lawyer.

After several months of negotiations, the company agreed to forgo the $5 million payment it would receive and to complete the integration work at no cost to the electric utility. In other words, the company would bear an expense of about $10 million. Fortunately, the company had sufficient cash to withstand this storm. However, the company's stock price was destroyed because of the one-time charge that was announced. This led to a hostile takeover attempt, which spurred the company to find a white knight to acquire it in order to defeat the move. But that's another story.

None of the senior executives in the company had any experience at entering contracts for systems integration. Further, the contract manager's experience had been in government contracts where equitable adjustments are often made when mistakes like this occur. The contract manager had tried to save a few thousand dollars on a $20 million contract by not having it reviewed by a lawyer. The CEO, not having any experience with systems integration contracts, did not insist on having the contract reviewed by a lawyer. This is an example of the typical entrepreneur's attitude toward saving pennies and losing dollars, or millions of them, by not taking the proper precautions.

Defaulting on Contracts

Many development-stage companies, when faced with the realization that an agreement they've entered into is defective or doesn't contain necessary terms that would have been added during a legal review, will seriously resist when the other side tries to enforce the agreement. It's almost as if an agreement is valid only if there are no problems but can be ignored when convenient.

I've also found that many companies realize early on they might not be able to comply with the terms of a given agreement, but they fail to advise the other party and don't try to negotiate some type of resolution to the developing problem. Instead, they wait until the company is in default and then attempt to argue that the agreement doesn't really mean what it says.

I tell my clients they should deal in good faith with the other party when they realize the company is likely to default under the agreement. I once worked with a company that had signed a five-year lease for a substantial amount of office space and within one year determined it would shut down this office as a consolidation measure. The company alerted me it was going to stop paying rent on the space because it had not been able to find a subtenant. I advised the company it would be unwise to simply stop paying rent and that it should meet with the landlord and negotiate a resolution of the lease. The CEO told me it was simply unfair for the landlord to enforce the lease since the company was no longer occupying the space. I could not believe what I was hearing.

Proactive Legal Reviews

In the example above, the company entered into the lease for five years without running the contract by an attorney. Instead, the company had a real estate agent review the agreement. The agent commented that the lease was standard for this type of space and this locale.

A lawyer reviewing the proposed lease surely would have recommended a means of terminating the lease early through some type of payment in the event that the company found it could no longer use the space. If this recommendation had been made, the CEO would have at least had to deal with the economics of the situation at that time rather than after the company had defaulted and no longer had any leverage in the negotiations.

There are many times when clients negotiate agreements and then seek legal review at the very last minute. The lawyer makes recommendations concerning inconsistent business points in the agreement and matters that should be in the lease. By that time, it's usually too late to actually negotiate these things even though they could easily have been negotiated had they been part of the original discussions with the other party.

This is a dilemma for most business people. When should an entrepreneur involve a lawyer in drafting an agreement – when the agreement is being negotiated, or after the basic terms have been set but before the definitive agreement has been drafted? There's no simple answer. However, the more a business person works with a lawyer on these matters, the more likely it is that he or she will involve the lawyer at the negotiating stage to make sure all points are covered. Most corporate and business lawyers have more experience with the business points that belong in an agreement than the person who is negotiating. Yet most business people don't accept this argument. It's another case of "you don't know what you don't know."

Large companies and governmental entities go to another extreme with respect to legal review of agreements. They have *everything* reviewed by the legal department. Legal review has become institutionalized in these organizations as part of the overall routine. Legal review by large companies or governmental organizations is part of the economies of scale they bring to the overall process of entering into agreements. They can have agreements reviewed very efficiently, usually by in-house lawyers, at the crucial time of the negotiations rather than simply at the end of the negotiations and in the drafting of the definitive agreement.

Members of the management team at a development-stage company often have never been involved in a lawsuit over a contract. In fact, most of them have never been involved in a significant contract dispute. Is it any wonder they don't understand the ramifications of breaching an agreement? Even those management members who have MBAs seldom have actual knowledge of the potential damages that might be involved if the company breaches a contract. When I explain the fundamental basis of damages in the event the company breaches a specific agreement, the management team members are usually astonished at how much money could be awarded to the other side.

I also frequently hear the expression, "A good lawyer can get us out of this contract." A person making that kind of statement is naïve. Lawyers can't get clients out of well-written contracts.

The Ethics of Honoring Contracts

There's a business ethics issue when a company makes promises in an agreement and then knowingly breaks them without recognizing the ethical obligation of notifying the other party and trying to work out a resolution before the breach occurs. Many executives I've dealt with simply don't accept that they have an ethical obligation to keep the promises they make in agreements. Even though I lecture these people about the business ethics involved, my words fall like water off a duck's back.

In **Chapter 8: Engaging in Unethical Behavior**, I talk about unethical conduct by top management. However, in that section I'm dealing with a different type of unethical conduct than the ethics of agreements. When a company, acting through its executives, knowingly breaches an agreement without attempting to resolve the matter before the breach, many other employees in the company understand that other types of promises made by these executives are not likely to be kept. This can create an atmosphere of distrust or give lower-ranking employees the idea they can engage in unethical conduct with no fear of consequences.

Sometimes development-stage companies will adopt a code of conduct they've copied from a large company. Usually, this code states that the company will honor its agreements. I think every company, large and small, should have a code of conduct stated in simple terms. It's a step in the right direction.

6

Giving Prospective Investors Financial Projections That Don't Comply with Generally Accepted Accounting Principles

or

"It's too expensive to have an accountant look over the financial projections in our business plan."

The founders of a start-up company planned to develop a miniaturized laser that would be used in biomedical laboratories. The device used proprietary technology invented by one of the founders. The entrepreneurs prepared a business plan to present to angel investors, using an off-the-shelf software program to prepare all but the financial portion. Then they created their own version of financial projections on an Excel spreadsheet.

Their three-year financial projections contained numerous accounting errors that were obvious to any person familiar with generally accepted accounting principles, or GAAP, as used in the United States. For instance, the receipt of investment capital was shown as income to the company. There was no provision for federal income taxes even though the projections showed a significant profit for the first year and thereafter. Also, the product development efforts were capitalized rather than accounted for as a current expense, even though it was highly uncertain such expenses would result in future income.

The business plan did not describe milestones the company intended to meet. Instead, the plan included a vague description of when the company would have a prototype of the laser and when it would hire a sales manager to begin selling the product. I understood enough about the laser business to know the founders would have to overcome several technical problems and would have to find several laboratories that would be willing to act as beta sites to evaluate the laser before it could go on the market.

In my discussions with the founders, they revealed they needed several parts for the manufacturing process that they'd have to order months in advance. They told me they'd ask the supplier of these parts to allow them to pay 90 days after receipt. They had no provision in the business plan for paying for these parts in advance, which the supplier was more likely to require.

The founders also told me they intended to raise the next round of financing from venture capital firms at a significantly higher valuation than the value they would place on the company in this angel round of financing.

When I saw the business plan, I quickly pointed out errors in the financial projections and the failure to identify milestones they needed to meet in order to raise money from venture capital investors. They argued with me that they'd seen other financial projections that handled these matters in the same manner and that, in their opinion, angel investors didn't pay attention to these projections anyway. They also argued that they didn't put milestones in the plan because they didn't want to make commitments to the investors they might not be able to meet.

I declined to take on this company as a client. Several months later, a member of a well-known investment group made up of angel investors told me the group had reviewed the business plan and had rejected it out of hand even though the members thought the product had merit. The investors knew the presentation of the financial projections was not according to generally accepted accounting principles and, therefore, distrusted everything in the business plan.

Financial Projections Are Important

Financial projections are an inherent part of raising capital. Without financial projections, no company can raise equity capital privately or publicly. When a company is trying to raise private capital, all prospective investors expect to see financial projections as well as past financial statements. When a company is raising capital publicly, the investment bankers want to see the projections even though the projections will not be disclosed, per se, to the public investors.

I see financial projections and business plans several times every week. Companies that have already gone through a rigorous capital-raising process already know most of the pitfalls I'm going to discuss in this section. Companies that have not yet gone through this process, such as raising several million dollars from venture capital firms, are likely to commit the mistake discussed here.

Development-stage companies seldom need a chief financial officer. Instead, they need a controller who can handle the company's accounting matters, such as accounts receivable, accounts payable and other functions. A controller usually has no experience as a chief financial officer in raising capital or dealing with investors. In the development stage, the CEO has to be the CFO.

Telltale Signs of Inadequate Projections

All business plans, by their nature, contain financial projections. Those written by many development-stage companies contain detailed projections for five years out, yet the company has no clue when or how large the revenues will be even three months out. This is downright silly. It makes sense for the company to show a model of what might happen if the company is able to achieve the projected revenues. However, it makes no sense for the company to have great detail in any set of projections beyond two years.

The biggest unknown for all development-stage companies is the revenue they will produce over the next 12 to 24 months. Usually there's no real way to determine the potential revenues for that period unless a development-stage company has or develops a substantial backlog, or group of orders waiting to be filled. It's been my experience that these companies seldom can develop a backlog that goes out for more than a few months.

Another largely unknown number is the money needed to complete development of the company's main product or service. Development-stage companies almost always grossly underestimate the money needed. Experienced investors know this and almost always double, at least, the dollars that will be needed to get the company into a revenue-generating mode.

Another area usually under-projected is the cost of sales and marketing. Engineers from a large organization often start a new company based on technology related to what they were working on in the big company. They estimate sales and marketing at 3 percent to 5 percent of revenues based on a rule of thumb they got somewhere.

First, most development-stage company founders don't understand the difference between sales and marketing and, therefore, grossly underestimate the dollars that will be needed. Second, they oversimplify the sales process or cycle for their product by underestimating the time from first contact with a potential customer to placement of an order. One test experienced investors apply to a set of financial projections is to look at the projected balance sheets. It's difficult to project balance sheets given the differences between GAAP treatments of the numbers versus cash flow. Most development-stage companies fail miserably in projecting balance sheets unless they use a one-size-fits-all software program that forces the company to put its numbers in a prepackaged format rather than in categories or a format that makes sense for the company.

Another test is to look for the net after-tax profits projected, or the profits after all taxes have been accounted for. I can't tell you how many companies come to me with projections that go down to the net pretax profits and carry those forward on the projected balance sheets as if taxes are never paid. This is an instant red flag to me and to any other qualified investor looking at the projections.

The other side of all of this is that some projections contain an incredible amount of detail because a qualified accounting person has prepared them. The detail is carried out beyond one year, beyond two years, often all the way to five years, even though the assumptions behind those details are likely to change significantly within three months. When I see a set of projections like this, I know the CEO of the company does not have a good sense for the dynamics of the accounting or cash flow or the future. No CEO should allow these kinds of projections to get out to prospective investors because they are immediately suspect.

Preparing Effective Financial Projections

Given the uncertainties and the mistakes usually made in financial projections for development-stage companies, why do investors even study these projections? One reason is that savvy investors can tell the founders' level of experience by reviewing them. It's refreshing to find a set of financial projections from a development-stage company that takes into account all of the things that I've said above. Unfortunately, it seldom happens.

It would be wise for development-stage companies to first introduce a set of financial projections by setting out the factors that influence the numbers the most. The first discussion is about the factors that influence revenues and why the revenues have been projected as they are. The second should be about the projected product development costs and factors that will influence them. The third is about expenses necessary to begin the selling process for the products in order to achieve the projected revenues.

A business plan that has this kind of discussion leading into the financial projections will get an A+ for its projections. Then financial projections can be made, often in generalities because everyone knows things will not go as they've been assumed.

Separately, the financial projections can show a headcount with compensation levels for various employees, which is always of interest to investors to make sure founders are not overpaying themselves during the development stage of the company.

The financial projections should also show wise use of the capital that will be received from the offering. For instance, there should be some discussion about minimizing capital expenditures by leasing equipment instead of purchasing it, or through other means. There should also be a discussion of when to incur sales and marketing expenses because those made before the company is able to deliver the product or service are usually wasted.

Development-stage company founders are often eager to see their product or service advertised in trade journals long before they're able to deliver it. Further, they often hire sales people and establish sales offices in different parts of the country before they even have something to sell. They just can't get the message that they need to focus on a limited market initially until they have customer traction.

I often advise companies to focus on only one region of the country to get started rather than project they will almost immediately establish sales offices nationwide. Since perceived opportunities rather than available resources drive development-stage companies, they're afraid they'll miss sales opportunities if they don't have sales offices throughout the country. Yet the better approach is to make sure they can provide service in-depth before they try to go out beyond the initial region.

Why Financial Projections Are Essential

Development-stage companies spend too little time preparing financial projections in a business plan. In large part, this is because the company has not done the planning that would lead to sound assumptions for its financial projections. This is a classic case of the company developing a business plan for raising money rather than for running the company. If the business plan is developed for operating the company, the founders will use much greater care in preparing the financial projections.

Founders of development-stage companies are often afraid to develop a business plan for running the company because that plan is likely to be much more conservative than a plan used for raising money. The founders are in for a rude awakening. When the company seriously misses the revenue goals set out in the plan for raising capital, the investors are unhappy. It's best to start off with an honest, accurate projection so there are no unnecessary surprises.

Founders have said to me many times, "If I use the operating plan, I'll never be able to raise capital." My response is, "Then you should not raise capital." This tends to get the company founders focused on what has to be done to prepare a business plan to be used for both raising capital and running the business.

7

Expecting the CFO to Be a Proponent of Aggressive Accounting

or

"Our CFO can always find a way to make our numbers meet expectations."

Carl, an engineer from a large defense company who had worked on laser guidance systems for several years, created a company called Laserpoint to manufacture and sell laser systems that could trim small wire leads on semiconductor chips. Semiconductor manufacturers already used this type of technology as part of an automated system to mount the chips onto printed circuit boards, but the current standard was to use large, expensive lasers. Carl knew he could make a version that would be much smaller and cost less.

Laserpoint received a large order for Carl's product based on a prototype he and his company developed. After learning about these orders, a small investment-banking firm in Denver approached Carl and offered to do an initial public offering for Laserpoint. The IPO was successful and Laserpoint became a publicly held company with its stock trading on Nasdaq.

Before going public, Laserpoint hired a chief financial officer who had been a manager at one of the major accounting firms. Although the CFO had a fair amount of experience at auditing small publicly held companies, he had never worked as a CFO reporting to a chief executive officer. He was eager to please the CEO, Carl.

After about a year, the stock's price fell below its original offering price and the company was under pressure to produce positive earnings per share. Near the end of the fiscal year's first quarter, about 18 months after the IPO, the CFO advised Carl the company would show a loss for the first quarter due, in large part, to a slowdown in shipments to the company's largest customer. The CEO became angry, blaming the CFO and other executives for failing to achieve this important milestone. He asked the CFO what could be done to show a profit for the quarter.

The CFO made several suggestions, one of which was to offer the company's largest customer extended payment terms if the customer took delivery of four more systems that month than planned. The marginal profit on the four systems would put the company into the black for the quarter. The CEO ordered the vice president of sales to approach the customer and make this offer. The customer accepted.

Under this arrangement, the additional revenues at the end of the quarter amounted to almost $1 million. Direct costs associated with the additional systems were about $300,000, so the added sales contributed almost $700,000 to the bottom line before taxes and made the company profitable for the quarter. The company's stock price rose more than 50 percent over the five trading days after these results were reported.

Later, when asked for the business reasons for this maneuver, the CFO had to admit the sole reason was to meet the projections for the quarter.

Was it ethical for the company to recognize the additional sales made to the large customer because of the special terms? No. The motivation for offering the special terms was solely to create profits at the end of the quarter. In effect, the company "borrowed" sales from the following quarter by moving them into the current quarter, hoping it could later find other sales to take their place.

The company did this several more times until a securities analyst asked the right question and discovered how the company was meeting its quarterly projected earnings per share. When the analyst confronted the CFO, the chief financial officer made excuses for the company's behavior. However, the securities analyst wrote a scathing report about the situation and the company's stock price hit a new low. A class-action lawsuit was filed against the company for fraud on the market so stockholders who had bought based on the false numbers could seek to recover their investments. The suit eventually was settled out of court. The CFO resigned and Carl took early retirement.

The Role of the Chief Financial Officer

This section applies primarily to small-cap, publicly held companies, or those that have numerous investors who are following the company's performance on a quarterly basis. Officers, directors or stockholders in development-stage companies might be interested in this section since a primary objective of most development-stage companies is to become publicly held.

The role of the chief financial officer has changed dramatically. Until about 10 years ago, CFOs were expected to be the conservative voice on the management team when it came to financial matters. They usually advocated conservative accounting. As the stock market approached a financial bubble in the late 1990s, the CFO for each publicly held company became the primary public spokesperson for his or her company.

Before the U.S. Securities and Exchange Commission adopted a rule requiring public disclosure of any matters discussed with securities analysts in order to provide investors with a level playing field, CFOs regularly held private conferences with these analysts and provided them with either financial projections for the next fiscal year or hints at those kinds of projections, depending on the games the CFOs and securities analysts played in these meetings. Securities analysts would then write up their reports and predict the financial results for at least several quarters.

It was a favorite trick of the analysts to ask a CFO to comment on a report they were about to publish. All CFOs quickly learned not to comment since their words would, in effect, be viewed as confirming the analysts' projections.

When SEC Regulation FD, or Fair Disclosure, went into effect in 2001, it caused great consternation among CFOs and securities analysts. Because of this rule, company officials cannot hold private conferences with securities analysts and companies are encouraged to provide revenue and earnings guidance for at least the next quarter and often for the remainder of the fiscal year. This gives the general public information that used to be provided only to the securities analysts. Although it's designed to prevent analysts from potentially abusing this information, it has created new opportunities for unethical acts.

Because the stock market became so sensitive to whether a company met the guidance it provided, CFOs came under intense pressure to make sure the actual results slightly exceeded the guidance they had provided. Is it any wonder some companies used aggressive accounting to achieve the guidance they had provided to the market?

Until recently, CFOs were no longer the voice of conservatism within the management team of a company. CFOs were expected to be "managers of earnings" to achieve the guidance the company provided to the market.

Companies now hold conference calls at least quarterly to discuss the performance of the company for the last quarter. These calls are usually open to the general public and the CFO is usually the principal spokesperson. My observation is that CFOs feel intense pressure to achieve the revenue and earnings projections they provide in these conference calls for the next quarter or fiscal year-end. Fortunately, the Sarbanes-Oxley Act – enacted in 2002 to hold companies more accountable and prevent scenarios like those that led to the downfall of companies such as Enron and WorldCom – is changing the role of the CFO. But the change is occurring slowly.

Conservative Accounting Policies

When the CFO is not the member of senior management who constantly recommends using conservative accounting, and when the CFO pushes the envelope on accounting rules to achieve the guidance given during the previous conference call, who fills the role today of being the proponent of conservative accounting in a publicly held company?

That falls to the audit committee. Some would argue this has always been the committee's responsibility. My observation is that audit committees used to rely on the CFO and the company's outside auditing firm to follow conservative accounting policies. Now, with the intense focus on audit committees caused by the accounting abuses that took place at Enron, WorldCom and other companies, each audit committee must, in essence, decide for itself whether conservative accounting practices are being used. This places a burden on each audit committee whose members, for listed companies, must be independent directors. By definition they are part-timers. How much time must an audit committee for a listed company spend on oversight? Has the audit committee been turned into an auditor of the auditor?

Somehow, boards of directors and audit committees must force CFOs back into the role of being the conservative person on the management team. Perhaps it means the CFO should officially report to the audit committee and not to the CEO. This would not sit well with CEOs.

Accounting Abuses

There are many lessons to be learned by the high-profile corporate accounting scandals that have occurred over the past several years. Let's review some of the major accounting issues that led to these scandals.

- **Recognizing revenue too early**. Companies have been tempted to recognize revenue before all the elements are in place to take certain transactions into the revenue category. What does this mean? Let's look at two examples. If a company sells a certain device and has no further responsibility for it after it's delivered, other than a standard warranty of replacement if the device is defective within a certain period of time, then revenue from a sale is recognized when the company has shipped the device to fulfill a customer's order. Under generally accepted accounting principles, or GAAP, it's OK to count the revenue at this point instead of when the company receives payment. When the device is shipped, an account receivable is created showing that the buyer owes the company money. The account receivable goes on the balance sheet as an asset. Since an asset has been created, the company recognizes revenue.

  On the other hand, if the company receives an order for a customized software product that must be designed specifically for the customer even though it uses some standard components developed by the company, then the company generally cannot recognize revenue until all of its obligations are completed under this order except for minor and customary warranty obligations. This applies even if the company receives full payment at the time the order is placed.

  Under the software example, the company would receive a cash payment in advance of the work and the cash would show up on the balance sheet as an asset with a liability showing for the customer deposit. No revenue is recognized by the company on the date cash is received. The company then customizes the software and installs it. If the customer must accept the installation and has the right not to accept it if it doesn't meet the customer's requirements, the company should not recognize revenues for the sale until the customer has given its approval after installation.

  Sometimes it's blurry about when acceptance takes place, and companies are tempted to recognize revenue early. Some companies try to recognize revenues up front by characterizing most of the payment received in advance as a non-reimbursable license fee rather than as a deposit on work to be performed by the company in the future. This is a dangerous area and has caused difficulty for many software development companies.

  If revenue is recognized earlier than permitted under GAAP, the company's profitability during that period is increased. If the revenue is recognized only after the work has clearly been done, future profitability is increased. Because of the focus the stock market places on the short term for publicly held companies, there is great temptation to recognize revenues early.

- **Deferring expenses**. It's also often tempting for companies to defer expenses. In effect, companies spend money on development or some other project, which the company then treats as an asset under the basic accounting view that revenues and expenses should be matched with respect to projects or developments. If the company has a great deal of confidence as well as a history of developing revenues from the investment in development, the company may properly under GAAP treat this expenditure as an asset and amortize it over revenues received in the future based on this development. However, this type of expense deferral must be reviewed carefully so as not to mislead stockholders and potential investors.

Conservative companies expense these kinds of developments as the costs are incurred. This causes an increase in expenses in the current quarter and a decrease in expenses in future quarters because these development expenses will not be amortized over future quarters.

One of the allegations against WorldCom is that it chose to capitalize certain expenses that should have been expensed over a period of time. As I understand it, WorldCom had excess fiber-optics capacity and had to perform maintenance on it, so it chose to capitalize part of the maintenance expenses. WorldCom justified this by saying the fiber optics capacity in question was not being used but would be used in the future. Therefore, by applying the simple view that expenses and revenues should be matched, WorldCom chose to defer the expenses until revenues developed through the use of the fiber-optic capacity in the future when these expenses would be amortized over time. However, there was great uncertainty over when the capacity would be used.

The effect: Deferring these expenses increased WorldCom's profitability in the periods when the expenses were deferred and would decrease the profitability at some time in the future as these expenses were amortized. This WorldCom example illustrates the complexities that come into play when accounting decisions are made.

New Financial Reporting Rules

The SEC has proposed new rules about disclosures publicly held companies make quarterly and annually in the management discussion and analysis section, or MD&A, of their financial reporting documents. Under the proposal, companies must explain major accounting issues and how they've dealt with them. If WorldCom had done this and thoroughly explained its reasoning behind capitalizing the maintenance expenses by showing what the results would have been if the expenses had not been capitalized, I suspect WorldCom would not be accused of failing to comply with GAAP.

I applaud the SEC for proposing that companies more fully disclose these types of items and the choices companies make along with the reasoning for those choices. If companies conscientiously do this in their MD&As, it's unlikely there will be major abuses like those that have occurred in the past over revenue recognition or deferral of expenses.

Choosing a CFO

In most publicly held companies, the chief executive officer selects the chief financial officer with little review of the selection process by the board of directors. This must change. One duty of the board is to bring wisdom to major decision-making. Selecting a CFO is one of the most important decisions a company can make. In almost all instances of major corporate failures to properly disclose the financial condition and operations of the company, the CFO is the person primarily responsible. The chief executive is often a driving force behind the CFO in these types of matters, but a qualified CFO would almost certainly have prevented the abuse.

Of course, under these types of circumstances, one qualification that's a must-have for a CFO is courage to take a potential "career-terminating action" by alerting the board of directors when the CEO applies pressure. This expression comes from one of the officers of Enron who blew the whistle knowing she would lose her position at Enron for doing so.

It might surprise people to know that most CFOs of publicly held companies are not certified public accountants. They usually have MBAs and only a small percentage of them are CPAs with auditing experience. Is this bad? I don't think so, provided they're capable of stepping back to apply "principles" and not seek ways to push the limits of complying with complex accounting rules.

Does an MBA teach a person how to apply principles rather than rules? Probably. But the CFO must have the ability to develop a vision along with the CEO that will add value for shareholders in the long term. This is the reason most CFOs of publicly held companies are MBAs rather than CPAs.

CFOs must have high personal ethical standards and have the courage to stand up to CEOs and other officers who are anxious to have them find ways under the accounting rules to improve earnings on a short-term basis or have the balance sheet appear healthier than it really is. Of course, it's very difficult to determine the ethical level of a CFO candidate when going through an interviewing process and a background check.

It can be argued that people who have been CPAs for most of their careers might not be qualified to be CFOs because they lack experience on the front line of negotiations for raising capital, handling mergers and acquisitions, and developing overall financial strategy.

The CFO's Influence

In small companies, most CFOs tend to be more like controllers who are not expected to develop a vision or overall strategy. The role of the controller is to focus on internal controls and on financial reporting from an accounting standpoint. The controller, however, is not simply a "bean counter," a term I often hear used by operating management to exclude the controller from the mainstream of strategic discussions among members of the management team.

For publicly held companies listed on the New York Stock Exchange, another exchange or Nasdaq, the Sarbanes-Oxley Act requires the company's auditing firm to report directly to the audit committee. This will have the effect of requiring direct interaction between the CFO and the audit committee without interference by the CEO. That has not previously been the case, with the CFO making reports to the board. This new arrangement provides the CFO with a safe harbor with the audit committee if the CEO or some other senior officer applies pressure to take an aggressive position about accounting issues. In the past, most audit committees have been almost entirely passive and have not provided this safe harbor. Clearly, the invisible hand of the audit committee will be felt not only on the CFO but also on the CEO.

A qualified CFO can have a dramatic influence on the long-term financial performance of a company if the CFO, the CEO and the members of the board of directors are brave enough to sacrifice the short-term to benefit the long-term. This usually requires extensive communication with shareholders, the stock market and securities analysts so everyone knows why the company is investing in the future by reducing short-term profits. It can be done.

I'm concerned that over time a sense of distrust might develop between the CFO and the CEO when it's perceived the chief financial officer reports to the audit committee and not to the chief executive. As the power of the audit committee becomes more obvious over time, this conflict must be resolved within each company. The role of the CFO has changed dramatically in the past 10 years and is about to change dramatically again over the next five years because of the expanded role of the audit committee.

8

Engaging in Unethical Behavior

or

"We can inflate our revenues for this quarter by making our distributors take early deliveries of our products and giving them longer payment terms."

John founded a company to make a laser that could be used to remove cataracts. John was a brilliant engineer and had developed a means to make the laser much smaller than others on the market. Other manufacturers had to water-cool their lasers because they produced so much heat due to inefficiency.

He found a small venture capital firm where one of the partners understood the significance of John's invention and the potential for using the laser for removing cataracts. The firm brought in two other venture capital firms and, together, they invested $4 million into John's company.

Within 12 months, the company had orders from several medical device distributors with a backlog of about $6 million. Based on this backlog, John and the venture capitalists approached a small investment-banking firm in Las Vegas, which agreed to take the company public.

The public offering went off like clockwork, and over the following 12 months, the stock price rose to more than double the initial public offering price. John and the venture capital firms were happy, and several brokerage firms began to cover the company by writing research reports about it.

Like most entrepreneurs, John was intense and placed a great deal of pressure on his executive officers to achieve the company's revenue and expense projections for each quarter. Regulation FD had not yet been adopted, and the company and securities analysts played games with each other as the securities analysts made projections of the revenues and earnings and then tried to obtain verification of the projections from the company's CEO or CFO. As was the case with many small publicly held companies, the securities analysts obtained the company's internally prepared financial projections one way or another.

John soon went through what other publicly held companies experienced: If the company missed the earnings per share projected by securities analysts, the stock price took a significant hit even though the actual performance of the company was better than that of the previous comparable quarter. John wanted to exceed the projections made by the securities analysts for each quarter by a small amount. He knew exceeding the projections by a large amount would not result in a significantly higher price for the stock but would set the target for the next quarter higher than the company's internal projections.

John implemented a bonus system for his executive officers based on meeting quarterly earnings-per-share targets. Since the revenues for each quarter had the greatest impact on earnings per share, the burden to produce the targeted revenues was very great on the vice president of sales. Further, the other executive officers placed internal pressure on the vice president of sales because they knew their own bonuses were dependent upon meeting the quarterly revenue targets

For each of the next five quarters, the company slightly exceeded the targeted earnings per share and continued to be a darling among the securities analysts. The vice president of sales earned bonuses for those five quarters in excess of twice his base salary. John and the board of directors were happy and, clearly, the vice president of sales was happy.

Almost all of the company's sales were to three large medical device distributors who sold directly to hospitals and to ophthalmologists who performed surgery in their offices. The distributors placed orders with the company in anticipation of the demand for these lasers, but the orders were cancelable on 30 days' notice.

The company had two salesmen in addition to the vice president of sales. There was no need for a large sales force since the number of customers was quite small. The salesmen often called directly on hospitals and ophthalmologists, in effect becoming salesmen for the distributors. As a result, the salesmen were in close touch with customers of the distributors and had a good "feel" for their buying attitudes.

One day both salesmen came to the vice president of sales to advise him that the company's primary competitor had announced a substantial decrease in the price of its units. While the company's laser was superior to the competitor's product, the reduced price would most likely have a temporary effect on sales. The company was going to announce improvements to its units in about six months and was considering a price decrease to meet the competitor's price, but the vice president of sales knew this would reduce the next term's revenues.

Both of the salesmen had commission arrangements that called for them to receive commissions within 30 days following the shipment of units they sold even though the company had not yet received payment for them. The company was comfortable with this arrangement because it was confident the three distributors would pay for the units they purchased.

As the end of the quarter approached, the vice president of sales realized that orders were behind and the company would not meet its revenue projections. At the same time, the two salesmen realized orders from hospitals and ophthalmologists to the distributors were slowing down and the number of units that would be shipped through this quarter would be less than projected. The salesmen approached the vice president of sales and offered a creative solution to this short-term problem.

They proposed to ask the distributors to issue purchase orders for more units than they probably would need for the next two quarters, with a side understanding that they would take delivery of the units before the end of each quarter but not be required to pay for them until they were actually resold by the distributors. The vice president of sales and the salesmen would not tell the company's chief financial officer or accounting department about the side agreement until the accounting department raised a concern about the level of accounts receivable, at which time they would tell the accounting department the sales department was offering 90-day payment terms to combat competition.

The vice president and salesmen were confident the slowdown in sales by the distributors was temporary and that the distributors would buy all of the units that were shipped "early" before the end of the company's fiscal year.

As you can guess, the weakness in sales by the distributors continued for the balance of the company's fiscal year and the "early shipments" came to light near the end of the fourth quarter. The vice president knew the company's auditors would discover that the distributors had a side letter saying they didn't have to pay for the units they had in inventory until they sold them. The vice president and the salesmen had "stuffed" the distribution channel in order to report higher sales in the first three quarters. The vice president tried to justify his conduct to the CEO, but the CEO knew the vice president had cheated.

The CEO immediately advised the board of directors, and the company issued a press release correcting the results for the first three quarters. Within three days, the price of the company's stock declined by 50 percent.

Late on Friday afternoon after the announcement had been made, the company's in-house counsel received a call from the Securities and Exchange Commission indicating that the SEC would make an informal investigation about the circumstances leading to the decline in the price of the stock. Although the company was not required to announce the informal investigation under SEC Rules, I advised the company to do so and to launch an internal investigation by outside counsel immediately. The company made this announcement on the following Monday. On Tuesday, a class-action lawsuit was filed against the company, its board of directors and the officers, alleging fraud on the market, a common theory at the time for class-action lawsuits.

The internal investigation revealed the special terms offered to the distributors. The vice president of sales denied any knowledge of the arrangement, but the two salesmen were prepared to testify that he participated with them as a way to make the revenue goals for the three quarters, which would trigger substantial bonuses.

The investigation by external counsel, which was my law firm, indicated the founder of the company had no knowledge of the channel stuffing arrangement. However, the bonus system the CEO had put in place was based on short-term, quarterly goals, which had the effect of putting the salesmen and the vice president of sales under enormous personal economic pressure. The board of directors terminated the vice president of sales and the two salesmen and advised the SEC that the company would fully cooperate in its investigation.

After about six months, without any explanation, the SEC discontinued its investigation, although it would not confirm the investigation was over. This was unusual but sometimes happens when the SEC is short on resources. In the meantime, the class-action lawsuit continued and was settled for several million dollars. The company was acquired before the final settlement of the suit, but that's another story.

The vice president of sales and the salesmen started down a slippery slope when they conceived the scheme to increase revenues at the end of the quarter and couldn't catch up. Clearly, the vice president and the salesmen engaged in unethical conduct. Had the SEC pursued the matter, they probably would have been charged with criminal violations of federal securities laws for falsely reporting revenues to make the reported earnings higher than they should have been.

Unethical Behavior by Executives

It should go without saying that ethical behavior in any company must start at the top with the CEO, with other executive officers and with the board of directors. Unfortunately, it's been my observation that just the opposite has been true in many companies.

Philip Crosby, a good friend and client of mine and one of the world's gurus on quality management, founded The Quality College in the late 1970s in Winter Park, Florida. The program taught three- and four-day courses for executives and managers from large companies. I always marveled at Phil's requirement that before anyone from a given company could attend The Quality College, the CEO had to go through the program first. Phil enforced this rule with some of the largest companies in the United States. He preached that quality starts at the top of a company and not at the hourly employee level. So it is with ethical behavior.

How can we explain the conduct of some CEOs and chief financial officers for publicly owned companies over the past several years? No doubt some CEOs and CFOs engaged in unethical behavior, usually involving accounting matters or loans to insiders or perks that were not reported as compensation in the proxy statements. Over the course of my career, I've seen all kinds of unethical behavior. Without exception, the people committing the unethical behavior didn't believe they were engaged in any wrongdoing. It came as a total surprise to each when he or she was accused of unethical behavior and, sometimes, prosecuted and convicted of wrongdoing.

In every instance, the executives involved had justified their behavior in some fashion, believing it was appropriate or that the financial benefit was well-deserved.

I don't know of any company that puts a prospective CEO or CFO through some type of ethical test, and I'm not aware whether any such test exists. Instead, the company checks the executive's references and relies on those in determining whether the candidate is viewed as an ethical person.

Unfortunately, many CEOs and CFOs change their way of thinking after the company becomes successful. It's ironic that companies experiencing the most success tend to breed wrongdoing by some executive officers. Perhaps the increased power executives gain as a company gets larger tempts them to engage in wrongdoing – although, as I've said, they don't believe they're doing anything inappropriate.

Another attitude develops: Many CEOs, especially if they founded the company, believe the board of directors works for them and not the other way around. Sometimes the CEO's attitude is more extreme and he or she sees the board of directors as a mere nuisance to be tolerated. This attitude is a breeding ground for wrongdoing in the future because the founder/CEO believes he reports only to himself.

Avoiding or Stopping Unethical Behavior

One of the primary roles of a company's board of directors, whether the company is large or small, is to establish ethical ground rules and to enforce them vigorously. When employees see a CEO or a CFO engage in wrongdoing, however small, every employee is given a license to engage in wrongdoing of at least the same magnitude.

Most executive officers who engage in minor unethical behavior don't realize that employees pick up on it quickly. The word spreads among employees, and inevitably some of them feel they're now authorized to engage in the same or worse behavior. Executive officers must realize the consequences of their actions and how these affect employees.

When the unethical behavior rises to the level of accounting fraud or embezzlement, some employees don't understand the nature of the wrongdoing and wind up actually aiding the executive officer, believing he knows what he's doing. Usually, large-scale accounting fraud can't take place without the participation of many people, some of whom are innocent participants. We saw this in the Enron case, and we've seen what often happens to whistle-blowers, or employees who go to authorities with their concerns when they spot wrongdoing. They get fired.

The Sarbanes-Oxley Act, passed in 2002 to strengthen controls in publicly held companies, contains provisions for protecting organizations against accounting fraud. One of those provisions requires the audit committee of the board of directors to have a procedure for whistle-blowers to provide information to the audit committee without the threat of retaliation. It's too early to tell how companies will implement this across the board, but it's a big step forward to prevent accounting fraud.

9

Creating or Tolerating Conflicts of Interest

or

"My daughter doesn't have any experience at being a marketing director, but I know she'll be loyal to me."

A construction contractor started a business that prefabricated small office buildings by casting the walls off-site and trucking them to the location. He raised almost $1 million from several investors who normally sought real estate deals. The company grew rapidly and soon had more than 50 employees. However, the founder insisted the company employ his two sons in senior management positions and his wife as the controller. The investors questioned this practice and finally confronted the founder after sales growth had flattened and the company started suffering losses.

Two of the investors decided to interview several key employees about the problems. The investors were horrified to learn that both of the founder's sons lacked qualifications for the positions they held but were paid significantly more than other senior managers. When the two investors confronted the founder about this, he argued that even though his sons were not the most qualified for the positions, he could trust them.

He also argued that he was the controlling shareholder in the company and had the right to employ his relatives. The investors threatened to sue the founder for failing to tell the board of directors about the compensation being paid to his sons and for breach of fiduciary duty in failing to hire qualified people for the positions filled by his sons. The pressure the investors put on the founder was so intense that the founder decided to sell the company rather than continue fighting with them. The investors were happy to sell the company.

Nepotism has no place in a company once the organization has investors. Nepotism is an automatic conflict of interest and often prevents a company that is not 100 percent family owned from achieving its full potential.

Identifying Conflicts of Interest

Conflicts of interest are difficult to deal with in all companies. I'm addressing those in which a member of management or a member of the board of directors has a personal interest in a matter that might be averse to the company's interests. It usually means the person will receive some monetary benefit at the expense of the company.

The first role of the board of directors on conflicts of interest is to put a mechanism in place that causes conflicts to surface. I've observed many times when conflicts of interest were present but not disclosed, usually by a member of management rather than an outside board member. Sometimes this is a result of dishonesty, but most of the time it's simply based on not understanding why conflicts of interest must be dealt with directly and at the highest level of the company. As counsel to the company, I have a duty to bring conflicts of interest to the attention of the board of directors if the CEO, CFO, or in-house counsel does not take appropriate action.

Every company, even small organizations, should adopt a conflict of interest policy and make sure each employee, officer and director understands it. Having a policy on conflicts of interest is often overlooked. So many times, the CEOs of small companies think people will know conflicts of interest when they see them. Unfortunately, this is seldom true.

State law requires that all members of the board of directors disclose any conflict they might have with respect to a matter being considered by the board. It's not enough just to abstain from consideration of the matter. Other members of the board are entitled to know about the conflict so they can understand the reason for abstention. All conflicts of interest at the board of directors level, no matter how small, should be dealt with by the board with full information. Of course, the best policy is for a member of the board of directors never to have a conflict.

Conflicts often arise when a member of the board is providing services such as consulting or legal counsel to the company. When this happens, the board should approve the director's terms of engagement for the services and be advised from time to time about money being paid to that person, or to his or her firm, and what types of services are being performed.

There are times when a member of the board will have an investment opportunity or other business opportunity the company would like to know about before the director takes advantage of it. A board member has a duty to bring this opportunity to the company first so the company can consider whether to take advantage of it. This is called the corporate opportunity doctrine.

Most directors seem to be conscientious about this. However, I've seen directors bring a business opportunity to the board and not describe it accurately, probably with the intention of discouraging the company from wanting to take advantage of it. Then when the company turns down the business opportunity, the director pursues it. Clearly, this is improper.

Conflicts of interest also arise at both officer and staff levels. Since most officers and employees are full-time employees, there essentially should be no conflicts of interest. Companies are wise to have a strict policy of forbidding conflicts of interest for full-time employees and for officers. We have now seen in the Enron matter how conflicts can arise and how the board of directors can mishandle them.

Employing Relatives

Whenever a relative of a senior executive or board member works for the company, there's a concern about the effects of nepotism. This is especially true for young companies. Employees invariably believe a relative of an executive officer employed by the company will receive special treatment. There is good reason for this belief. Relatives usually do receive special treatment.

Entrepreneurs often hire relatives to work for their companies. Whenever I have a chance to talk to companies where nepotism is flourishing, I always make fun of the situation but hope they get the point. I often say, "The likelihood of a relative of yours being the most qualified person to serve in that position from a skill, education and experience viewpoint is essentially zero."

Why do company founders and other executives cause the company to hire relatives? Usually, I hate to say, it is a clear matter of selfishness by the founder or executive officer wanting to do a favor for a relative. If the relative is the spouse of the founder or executive, it usually means the driving reason is to increase family income. Those founders or executive officers who are not motivated into nepotism by selfishness are driven by a form of paranoia. They don't trust others in various positions and want to have relatives in place because they think they can trust them. In other words, they identify trust as the principal qualification for the job. They desperately want people who will be loyal to them.

I have served as counsel to many companies where the founders believed they were entitled to employ their relatives as one of their perks. These same founders thought they were granting a favor to investors by letting them get involved in the company. This is a bad sign for investors.

When venture capital firms invest a company, one of their due diligence items is to find out whether the company employs relatives of any of the founders or executive officers. If relatives are employed in low-level positions such as a summer job for a college student, investors are not concerned. However, if a relative holds a key position, investors are very concerned.

If the investors are angels rather than venture capital firms, they seldom voice their concern before making the investment for fear they will upset the company founders. Whenever I represent angel investors, I advise them the time to complain about nepotism is before making the investment, not after.

Some companies adopt anti-nepotism policies and strictly enforce them. However, if nepotism is already present in a company, it's difficult for the company to eliminate it.

What Conflict Looks Like

Let me give examples of other types of conflicts that develop:

- A member of the board of directors asks the CEO to offer a job to his daughter who recently earned an MBA from the state university. The CEO tells the vice president of sales to hire this person. The vice president objects but does it anyway. Neither the CEO nor the director discloses this request to the board of directors.
- A member of the board has an investment in a small start-up organization the company is considering as a significant supplier of certain materials. The CEO knows of the director's interest in the company, but no disclosure is made to the board.
- As part of its strategic plan, the company has identified a certain technology it wants to develop. A board member is offered the opportunity to make an investment in a start-up developing the same technology. The director makes the investment and does not advise the company's board about the possible investment opportunity.
- A director asks the CEO to have the company make a significant con-

tribution to a local charity to show the company is a good corporate citizen. The CEO knows the director is on the board of the charity. No disclosure of the company's intent to make this contribution is made to the company's board of directors.

- A member of the board is a friend of the founder of a small technology company that wants to be acquired. The director suggests to the CEO that the company explore an acquisition of this small entity. The company makes the acquisition with the approval of the board. The director fails to disclose to the board that the founder of the smaller company agreed to pay him a significant fee for arranging the acquisition.
- A director agrees to support the position of the company's founder, who is also a member of the board, if the founder grants the director an option on a portion of the founder's stock. They make the deal and the director consistently votes the same way as the founder on many controversial matters. The director and the founder do not disclose the existence of the stock option granted by the founder to the other directors. This is most likely to happen in a company that is still privately held. If the company were publicly held, each officer and director would be required to answer questionnaires about beneficial ownership of stock, including options.

As you can tell from the previous list, conflicts of interest generally develop with the full knowledge of the person who has the conflict. Further, when conflicts are not disclosed, it's because the person knows there is a high probability the board of directors will not approve the transaction. Otherwise, a director will readily disclose a conflict of interest.

My experience has been that most directors do disclose conflicts. Often, they go overboard to disclose matters that could only remotely be viewed as a conflict. However, I've experienced each one of the conflicts from the previous list, learning about it long after the conflict should have been disclosed to the board.

10

Thinking It's Easy to Hire and Fire Key Executives

or

"I can tell within a few minutes whether to hire a person I'm interviewing for an executive position."

Bob had been thinking about starting his own company for some time. He quit his high-paying position as vice president of marketing for a computer peripheral manufacturer and purchased a small Central Florida company for several hundred thousand dollars.

Bob was excited about the prospects for this company and came to me for advice on raising $1 million from individual investors to launch an aggressive marketing program. I recommended he sell convertible preferred stock to investors and helped him prepare an offering memorandum and term sheet with which to approach investors. Because of his reputation in the area, he was able to quickly raise the money he needed.

Bob's company had a patent on a spray nozzle with unique characteristics that made it ideal for applying a certain insecticide. The company's founder had invented the device but had not been successful at finding large customers. Bob's strategy was to develop a portable machine and market it to restaurants, which could use it to spray their dining and kitchen areas. Rather than sell the nozzle to companies that made similar spray machines, he would sell the entire machine through restaurant equipment distributors.

The patented device could break a liquid spray into droplets 1,000 to 10,000 times smaller than those produced by a standard nozzle. This was significant because an insecticide called Pyrethin, a natural chemical derived from African daisies, was expensive. Yet it was especially effective for use in restaurants because it was deactivated by light. If restaurants could periodically spray for insects at night, the chemical would be deactivated by morning. Only a few molecules of Pyrethin were required to touch an insect to kill it. Standard spray nozzles produced droplets 1,000 times larger than necessary to do the job.

I was intrigued by the nozzle technology and so were the company's investors. Bob would serve as chairman and chief executive officer of the company. He had substantial experience in marketing and sales but none in manufacturing or operations. He needed to hire a president and chief operating officer whose experience filled in the gaps in Bob's background.

Bob placed an ad in the local newspaper for a person with experience overseeing a machine shop type of operation and received more than 100 résumés. He hired a 35-year-old man who had worked as a supervisor for 10 years in operations at a large manufacturing company that had a machine shop set-up. Within three months, Bob realized he'd made a mistake because his director of operations had no experience at dealing with suppliers and couldn't carry out a quality control program. It was an easy decision for Bob to make to terminate him.

Feeling burned, Bob turned to a friend, Jim, who was vice president of manufacturing for a company that made modems. The two had been friends for years, and their wives were close, too. Jim had a business degree and had started working for the modem manufacturer as the assistant controller. He had a strong background in cost accounting and had worked his way up the career ladder over the course of 10 years. As vice president of manufacturing, he was mainly responsible for scheduling production runs, meeting delivery schedules to customers, purchasing parts and keeping direct labor costs to a minimum. He relied on a vice president of human relations to deal with employee problems.

Bob asked Jim to be president and chief operating officer. Jim told Bob his salary requirements and Bob agreed to meet them even though the pay rate was significantly higher than he'd had in mind. He also agreed to grant a stock option to Jim for roughly 10 percent of the outstanding stock in the company and to vesting one-third up front and the balance over two years as long as Jim was in continuous employment with the company.

Bob couldn't conduct a thorough background check by asking Jim's current employer about his performance for the obvious reason that Jim had not announced his intention to leave. Bob felt comfortable with Jim and sure he could trust his friend to be loyal. Besides, Bob needed to fill the COO spot quickly because two members of the board of directors who represented the investors were pressuring him to get manufacturing under control.

Over the next several months, Bob began feeling uneasy about having hired his friend because he was getting complaints from suppliers and employees that Jim was heavy-handed. Also, the company was plagued with interruptions in production caused by supplier problems, and distributors were complaining about obvious quality concerns with the spray machines. Any time Bob asked Jim about these issues, Jim was defensive. Jim said Bob didn't understand how difficult it was to solve these problems. At every meeting of the board of directors, Jim would give an operations report that glossed over the issues, so the two directors representing the investors were not aware of them.

This situation continued for about 18 months after Jim started with the company. Bob called me and asked whether we could meet to discuss a problem he was having. When we met, he explained to me that Jim was simply not working out. Against my advice when he hired Jim, Bob had negotiated a three-year employment agreement that could not be terminated "for cause" based on poor performance. Bob could terminate Jim only if he committed a crime or disobeyed written instructions from the board, or under other circumstances that were not applicable.

I asked Bob whether he had confronted Jim over these matters. He admitted he had not, and he felt guilty he hadn't given Jim any warning about the possibility he would be fired. Bob was near tears as he told me how difficult it would be to terminate Jim because of their social activities together. He'd been worrying for three months. In the past several weeks, Bob was waking up at night agonizing about what he would say to Jim to terminate him. He said he realized now that signing a three-year employment agreement with his friend had been a serious mistake.

Bob asked me whether there was any way he could get out of paying Jim for the remaining term of the three-year contract. I told him "No." He didn't like my answer. I wanted to say "I told you so" but knew it was not the right thing to say at the time.

I did tell Bob that Jim had a duty to mitigate his damages by finding comparable employment in the area. If he did, the compensation he received from his new employer would offset the compensation Bob's company would have to pay through the end of the three-year contract. Bob said Jim had no incentive to find comparable employment. He could simply go to the beach for about 18 months. I advised him to offer an incentive by agreeing that if Jim found other employment at a similar salary level, the company would continue to pay him for the balance of the contract in an amount equal to 25 percent of his previous pay rate. In other words, Jim would make 25 percent more than he was making at the company for the remainder of the three-year contract by finding a comparable job. Bob suddenly perked up.

I then said, "Bob, I've terminated executives many times on behalf of companies. Would you like me to be the one to tell Jim he's terminated and give him a termination letter setting out the incentive for him to find other employment?" Bob was relieved and quickly accepted my offer.

The next morning, I met with Bob in his office to finalize the termination letter. Bob called Jim and asked whether the two of us could meet with him in Jim's office. I told the COO his employment was terminated effective immediately and that we hoped he would meet with his employees before leaving to ensure an orderly transition. I told him, simply, the company needed to find someone to take his place who had more experience dealing with suppliers and other operating matters and that it was in his best interest to find another position. I gave him the termination letter and asked him to read it.

Jim expressed shock that we would take this action. He told Bob he couldn't understand how his good friend could do this to him. I could tell Bob wanted to respond, but I interrupted and told Jim this was very hard for Bob to do and that the company's board of directors was behind Bob in this decision. I told Jim if he had any questions about the termination letter, he could talk to me. I would stay in the company's conference room for the next hour. At that, I motioned to Bob and we both left Jim's office.

We went back to Bob's office. I asked Bob to call his wife to tell her what had occurred since she would most likely hear from Jim's wife within the next few minutes. Bob called his wife and explained what had taken place. She was not surprised since Bob had confided in her over the past year about the problems Jim been causing.

Jim hired a lawyer who called me the next day threatening to bring a lawsuit on behalf of Jim for wrongful termination of employment. I told him we were honoring Jim's employment agreement and that the employment agreement gave us the right to terminate him without cause. I reminded him about a provision in the contract that if there were a lawsuit, the prevailing party would be entitled to recover reasonable attorney's fees from the other party. I told him if he brought a lawsuit, the company was highly likely to prevail and his client would end up paying the company's attorney's fees of $50,000 to $100,000.

Immediately after this telephone call, I sent Jim's lawyer a letter summarizing our conversation and reiterating the probable exposure Jim would have for attorney's fees ranging from $50,000 to $100,000. I sent this letter knowing that Jim's lawyer would have a duty to provide a copy of it to Jim. This letter was a means by which I could communicate directly to Jim. Otherwise, as a lawyer, I cannot communicate directly with another lawyer's client without that lawyer's permission.

After a few days, Jim's lawyer called me to say Jim would accept our offer contained in the termination letter. He also would fully comply with the terms of his employment agreement, which provided that he must turn over all company documents in his possession and must be available to the company to answer questions during the transition period after his termination.

Bob took over the COO position temporarily and hired an executive placement firm to find a qualified replacement for Jim. About three months later, Bob hired a COO with significant experience, including purchasing. The company flourished over the next few years and was acquired by a much larger organization, making Bob and his investors happy.

Hiring and Firing Key Employees

Bob made two classic mistakes. First, he hired a friend for a key position without digging into his friend's qualifications. Second, even though he knew Jim was not working out for more than 12 months, he couldn't muster the courage to fire him. Almost every entrepreneur I've dealt with is too quick to hire key employees and not quick enough to fire them when they don't work out.

It's extraordinarily easy for development-stage companies to make mistakes in hiring and firing key employees. There are several reasons for this. The founders usually don't have much experience in interviewing and hiring key employees. Further, the pool of potential key employees in a given geographic area is usually limited. Also, once key employees are hired, founders have great difficulty firing them because of the personality traits of entrepreneurs.

One of this book's themes is that CEOs, whether they're founders of development-stage companies or executives in small-cap publicly held companies, "don't know what they don't know." Most entrepreneurs will say, "I understand there are things I don't know, but I can hire people who do know." As easy as this is to say, it's hard for an entrepreneur to put this into practice.

The only way for company founders to overcome the "you don't know what you don't know" syndrome is to hire people who are highly experienced in those areas in which the founders have no experience. However, this is only the first step. The next, the hardest step, is to accept what the new person has to say about his or her own area of expertise. This means founders must quickly develop a sense of trust in the expertise of key employees.

One of my observations is that most entrepreneurs have a sense of paranoia. They believe everyone is out to take advantage of them. This attitude makes it difficult for an entrepreneur to trust that the key employee is an expert in his or her area.

Limiting the Scope of the Search

It would be wonderful if all entrepreneurs could accept what they don't know and seek out key employees, consultants and advisors to provide the missing knowledge and experience. However, even if the entrepreneur can cross this hurdle, finding a qualified key employee is extraordinarily difficult for development-stage and small-cap companies.

Most of these companies are reluctant to seek executives or key employees outside their geographic area because of the cost involved and because it almost always means they must hire an executive placement firm to do the job. Very few development-stage and small-cap publicly held companies are willing to pay the fees of qualified executive placement firms because they don't place great value on the services they provide.

Most development-stage companies simply put out the word among their friends and perhaps run an advertisement in the local newspaper or use several internet services. They notify various employment firms that they're looking for a person with certain qualifications and are willing to pay a commission if that person is found, but they're not willing to pay any front-end fees. The company is immediately deluged with résumés of non-qualified people because there's no incentive for these employment firms to pre-qualify potential candidates. Someone has to weed through the applications.

Because the company often has waited well beyond the time when this key employee was needed, the company feels under a great deal of pressure to hire someone to fill this slot. This leads to the company hiring a person who is less qualified than someone it could have found if the company had been patient and used a more effective process.

Interviewing Poorly

Even if a qualified candidate is found accidentally, the interviewing skills of the entrepreneur are usually abysmal. Instead of trying to determine whether the candidate possesses the proper qualifications for the key employee position, the entrepreneur spends 90 percent of the interview time selling the candidate on the company. While that's a necessary aspect of the hiring process, it shouldn't dominate the interview.

I attribute the poor interviewing skills of entrepreneurs to a lack of experience. Throughout my career, I've dealt with only a handful of entrepreneurs who had prior experience at hiring key employees and the interviewing skills necessary to smoke out the candidates' qualifications.

Entrepreneurs tend to act impulsively. They defend this by saying they're rapid decision-makers. However, most would rather hire a key employee on gut instinct than use a thorough process such as interviewing candidates, having them meet with members of the board of directors, and thoroughly checking out their employment history and references.

Hiring the Wrong People

Because of an ineffective hiring process, most young companies find themselves bringing in key employees who can't grow with the company. Some entrepreneurs say the people who should be key employees in a company's development stage are usually not people who can be key employees in a larger company because they don't accept authority well. I will have to admit I've seen this often with key employees in development-stage companies.

Entrepreneurs actually admire this trait of not accepting authority well because they possess it themselves. In addition, they tend to hire people who share their own characteristics. The board of directors of development-stage companies can help entrepreneurial founders overcome these tendencies and hire key employees through an effective, well-thought-out process.

Refusing to Pay Competitively

There's another major hurdle all entrepreneurs must overcome. They typically have little or no knowledge of the competitive compensation rates in their geographic area for the types of key employees they intend to hire. Further, they have no clue about salaries for similar key employees in areas outside their region. Entrepreneurs are often shocked by the compensation qualified candidates are seeking even when the company is in a development stage.

Entrepreneurs universally believe key employees should sacrifice part of their expected compensation in exchange for stock options in a development-stage company. As I often advise boards of directors for these companies, if you expect the candidate to pass an intelligence test, the one who accepts this logic fails.

The days are long gone when a qualified key employee will take a cut in compensation in exchange for a stock option to join a development-stage company. In fact, it's almost the other way around. Given the huge number of companies that have failed over the past several years, candidates for key employee slots are likely to ask for higher compensation as a form of a risk premium. They view stock options as an incentive, but with a low probability of ever having significant value.

Entrepreneurs must deal with this. Too many times I've seen them disregard qualified candidates for key employment slots because of the compensation level the candidate requested even though the candidate presented information on the prevailing rates for this position in the geographic area. When this happens, it's a case of saving pennies and squandering dollars.

Shying Away From Firing

Even when a development-stage company has engaged key employees using some type of effective process, it's unavoidable that one or more of them will not work out. As hard as it is for an entrepreneur to hire qualified key employees, it's more difficult for an entrepreneur to fire them.

Most company founders don't have the discipline to provide an honest assessment of performance to each key employee. Instead, they find ways to praise them, and when it comes time to terminate them for failure to perform, the key employees are surprised. Usually, it's as much the founder's fault the employee did not perform up to expectations as it is the fault of the employee.

Another reason that often leads to the need to terminate a key employee is that a sense of trust didn't develop between that person and the entrepreneurial founder. Without this element, the key employee will sooner or later have to go.

Once the founder decides a key employee needs to be let go, he or she usually fails miserably in executing the termination. I've been called in many times to sit with founders of development-stage companies while they fire key employees. The founder hates the thought of confronting this employee knowing he or she probably has no idea what's about to happen. The founder feels guilty for never having given a true performance review to this employee or advised the employee of specific things that need to be corrected. Nevertheless, once the termination decision has been made, it usually can't be reversed.

When I perform this "service," the founder asks the employee to come into his office, where I'm waiting. In development-stage companies, all employees know the company's lawyer. I immediately advise the employee that he or she is being terminated and the company is offering a severance package. I hand the employee a letter from the company signed by the CEO stating that he or she is terminated and setting out the severance offered. I keep the explanation for the termination as short and simple as possible. Typically it's something such as, "Things have not worked out between you and the company."

I advise the employee to coordinate the final arrangements with a designated employee, or the company's human resources manager if it has one. The employee is usually shocked and wants more information about the reasons why he or she is being terminated. I decline to get into that discussion and stay with the simple statement I previously made. Then the founder and I leave the room.

Every entrepreneur I've known loses a great deal of sleep over terminating a key employee. The entrepreneur is often a nervous wreck for days beforehand. I know I give entrepreneurs a sense of relief when I take on the role of delivering the bad news to the employee.

There are, of course, times when the key employee must be terminated "for cause." Most of the time when this happens, the reason is clear. It's usually a failure to live up to performance expectations. Sometimes it's for misbehavior in the form of sexual harassment, gross abuse of an expense account, or outrageous behavior outside the office. If the person has an employment agreement, the company must be careful to stay within the definitions of termination for cause contained in the document.

Ineffectively Negotiating an Employment Agreement

Experienced executives who are hired by development-stage companies usually insist on having employment agreements and getting them reviewed by their lawyers. One immediate response from the executive's lawyer is to make the reasons "for cause" objective rather than subjective. This almost always means a failure to perform will *not* be a basis for termination with cause. Many times, the company is so eager to get the executive that it's willing to agree to terms that are almost impossible to be used later in firing the employee for cause. In these instances, I always advise the company to have a right to terminate without cause through the payment of some reasonable severance. That way the company can terminate the executive simply by making an economic judgment concerning the payment of the severance rather than try to justify a termination for cause.

11

Electing Directors Who Won't Ask Hard Questions

or

"If I press the CEO too hard, I won't be elected to the board next year."

Bryan founded a consulting firm that specialized in teaching middle management of companies how to avoid sexual harassment claims. Reducing these kinds of claims can save a company a great deal of money. Yet most companies do a very poor job of training their middle managers on how to avoid them.

Bryan's company remained small for the first three years. Then, through a stroke of luck, Bryan met the CEO of a large retail company who complained that his organization seemed to have an unusually large number of sexual harassment claims. The organization hired Bryan's company to teach more than 1,000 middle managers on how to avoid these claims.

Part of the program was the use of written materials Bryan's company had prepared. Not only middle managers but all employees received written materials from Bryan's company. There were more than 100,000 employees. Bryan charged more than $30 per employee for the materials, plus $10,000 for each of more than 100 two-day seminars for the middle managers.

Bryan's company had penetrated one of the largest retail organizations in the country. Using this customer as a reference, Bryan's firm saw its sales take off. Bryan was approached by several investment bankers to go public. His company had an initial public offering and the stock steadily rose over the next two years as the organization continued to grow.

As part of the process of going public, Bryan was advised to put at least three independent directors on his board. He appointed three friends of his to the board, each the current CEO of a company. However, Bryan wanted to make sure he maintained control of the board, so he appointed his son and two of his senior managers as directors. Counting Bryan, the inside directors outnumbered the independent directors four to three.

The board held quarterly meetings, each lasting about two hours. Routine reports were given and none of the board members asked hard questions about the changing nature of the market for the company's services. One reason for the lack of hard questions was that the so-called independent directors were friends of Bryan's and felt honored to be on his board. Also, the independent directors were paid fees that were significantly higher than those usually paid to directors at companies of similar size.

I attended all meetings of the board. I was amazed none of the independent directors asked difficult questions of Bryan or any of the executives. Yet, it was becoming clear the market was changing for the types of services the company provided and that it was becoming difficult for the company to get new large customers. The company's customer base was changing from large organizations to small ones, and the cost of getting new customers was increasing rapidly.

Bryan discouraged the independent directors from asking questions, snapping at anyone who tried. He said the company was changing with the market and that none of the independent directors understood the business. None of the independent directors wanted to challenge Bryan because they wanted to continue serving. About three years after the initial public offering, with the stock price slightly lower than the initial offering price, Bryan was approached by another publicly held consulting company to be acquired. The acquisition price was slightly higher than the price of the stock at the time, but Bryan was tired of being a publicly held company and wanted to be acquired. Bryan called a special meeting of the board to consider the offer. He didn't want the independent directors to oppose this deal, so he gave them only summary information before the meeting. At the meeting, he made a brief presentation and then asked the company's investment banker to make a brief presentation. Bryan asked for questions and not one of the independent directors came forward.

I needed to make sure the directors considered the pros and cons of the acquisition even though they didn't seem to be interested in any reasons not to do the deal. I made a presentation outlining reasons to do the deal and reasons not to do the deal. I made sure my PowerPoint slides became part of the minutes of the meeting. The acquisition took place with the company's stockholders receiving shares in the other consulting firm in a tax-deferred exchange of stock.

Within one year, the value of the stock received by Bryan's stockholders was one half what it was at the time of the acquisition. In hindsight, there was little synergy between the two companies and the price of the stock reflected the difficulty the bigger company had in assimilating Bryan's company into its culture. Had the independent directors had the courage to ask questions about the rationale behind the acquisition, the shallowness of Bryan's thinking and the lack of synergy probably would have been obvious. Perhaps Bryan would have looked for another acquirer, which would have led to a better long-term result for the stockholders.

Identifying What to Ask

What are the hard questions? I could take the easy route and say directors will know the hard questions when they see them. This would be too simple. Hard questions are those the CEO or the CFO don't want the outside directors to ask. That definition isn't helpful either, is it? I've been at board meetings where an outside director, near the end of the meeting, asked the CEO, "Are there any questions we should have asked but didn't?" Does anyone seriously think the question the CEO comes up with in response to this question is going to be one of the hard questions?

Directors should expect management to explain any differences in the actual performance of the company versus the projections. These explanations should be in the information packages directors receive. If the explanation is not satisfactory, directors should ask for a better explanation before the meeting, if possible, so as not to take up precious meeting time. These types of questions are not usually the hard questions.

It takes homework and careful listening to be able to ask hard questions. When the company takes an action that is inconsistent with the company's strategy, the action should be questioned. When the answer to a question or the explanation of a matter doesn't make common sense, the director has probably stumbled onto a hard question that needs to be asked. However, hard questions are not micromanagement questions. Hard questions must be reserved for significant matters.

For an outside director, a good thing to do in preparation for a board meeting is to call each of the other outside directors to see if they have any concerns. Often, an outside director will express concerns to another outside director before a meeting that he or she will not express at the meeting.

Lawyers for most publicly held companies are preparing boilerplate questions audit committee members should ask of the auditor and the company as well as questions directors should ask at board meetings because of the Sarbanes-Oxley Act, enacted in 2002 to hold companies more accountable and prevent scenarios like those that led to the downfall of companies such as Enron and WorldCom. These questions, because management knows they will be coming, will not be hard questions. I'm concerned boards and audit committees will get caught up in the process caused by the Sarbanes-Oxley Act and not focus on the substance of potential problems.

When to Ask Hard Questions

Anytime a major acquisition by the company is proposed to the board for approval, there's a great opportunity for hard questions. Based on my experience and reading accounts of how many companies approve mergers or acquisitions, boards are usually guilty of going along with management's recommendation and the analysis of the company's investment banker without questioning the wisdom of the acquisition. Too often, a board will discuss an acquisition at one board meeting, receive an analysis from management a few weeks later, then have a special meeting by telephone to approve the acquisition after hearing from the company's investment banker about the fairness of the acquisition from a financial viewpoint. Talk about the outside directors being steamrolled!

The same thing often happens when a company is considering being acquired by another company. If the management is in favor of the acquisition, the analysis showing the benefits and risks to the company's shareholders will almost always be biased toward the acquisition. The outside directors in this case have a special duty to the shareholders to step back and make sure the acquisition makes common sense.

Outside directors need to muster the courage to ask hard questions whenever they become obvious. This is easy to say but hard to do. Outside directors always have to keep a balanced relationship with the CEO, the CFO and the other board members. If the outside director is too adversarial, the other board members and the CEO will soon ignore him or her. But there should be a healthy tension between the outside board members, the CEO and the inside directors.

The Role of the Board

People should not serve on a board unless they have a clear understanding with the CEO and the other directors that they'll ask hard questions and expect to be supported by the rest of the board. An outside director has to overcome the fear that he or she will ask a dumb question, thinking of it as a hard question. This will happen. However, an outside director can't allow this feeling to interfere with asking future questions.

If a member of the board or the CEO ever tries to discourage an outside director from asking hard questions, the outside director should immediately report this to the other board members. Hopefully, the other board members will be outraged and require the CEO or director to give a full explanation. No director should ever allow something like this to happen.

Asking a hard question is difficult. It's not easy to determine what the hard question is, and it's difficult to muster the courage to ask it. However, an outside director who has a reputation for asking hard questions will single-handedly create an invisible hand over the management team and, hopefully, prevent the management from making dumb decisions.

12

Allowing Board Members To Micromanage the Company

or

"You could have bought Gateway notebooks for $2,000 each instead of HPs for $3,000."

The eccentric but brilliant engineer who founded High Lumens Corp. specialized in optics and had been fascinated for many years with large-screen displays. At the time, manufacturers found it difficult to make a display system that could project images on a flat screen in a conference room with ordinary lighting. Large-screen displays had to use curved screens to focus the light, which meant viewers had to sit near the centerline of the screen to see the image. If the display system could produce more light output, the screen could be flat, creating a much wider viewing area. It also could be easily viewed in ambient light, unlike the old systems that required viewers to sit in a dark room because of low light output.

The founder had invented a means of significantly increasing the amount of light output from a custom-made version of a cathode-ray tube, the same device used in television sets. He also had found a way of using liquid to cool the face of the screen in front of the cathode-ray tube. That way the heat from the increased energy that was required for higher light output would not fry the phosphorous on the screen.

Many market commentators were predicting videoconferencing would soon take off, but the low light output of display systems remained an obstacle. The company's display system seemed to overcome that. However, the company faced several problems. It had to buy its custom-made cathode-ray tubes, manufacture the control system circuitry and cooling system, and assemble the large-screen display units. Long lead times for parts would require significant cash commitments. There also was no clear channel of distribution to customers. It would be expensive for the company to employ its own direct sales force.

The company contacted a venture capital firm, and one of the partners at the firm contacted me. After the two of us met with the company's leadership team, the company engaged me as its counsel to assist in the venture capital transaction. The venture capital firm brought in several other VC firms and the company sold series A convertible preferred stock to them in the first round of financing.

The board of directors was expanded to include the partner who asked me to visit the company and partners from two of the other VC firms. One of these partners, David, had previously been a faculty member in the MBA program of one of the Ivy League colleges. He had very recently joined his VC firm and this was one of his first investments. The partner in the other firm was a retired Marine Corps general who'd held a major command position before retiring. He loved the thought of having these display systems in the Pentagon.

Part of the VC deal was that the company would find an experienced CEO to replace the founder, who would become the chairman. Within about three months, the company found a qualified executive who was hired as the new CEO. I told him he probably had a honeymoon period of about three months before the company's founder would try to undermine him. I also warned him that David and the general might try to micromanage the company from the board level. He had been the CEO of another company and had experience in dealing with a board of directors. However, he had no experience in dealing with directors like David and the general.

As is customary with a company that receives its first round of venture capital, the company held monthly board meetings. During the very first one after the new CEO started, David announced at the beginning that the sole purpose for him at every board meeting was to decide whether the CEO should keep his job. I was in attendance at the board meeting as usual. The CEO and I looked at one another and laughed, thinking David was joking.

At the same meeting, the general dug into financial statements, sales reports and manufacturing problems in such detail that the meeting took more than six hours. David joined in and resonated with the general. The other directors didn't know what to think. The new CEO was shell-shocked. The founder blamed the new CEO for every problem that was identified, even though the CEO had been on board for less than a month.

Every monthly meeting after that was the same. David and the general questioned the CEO on every decision, criticizing him on 50 percent of them. By the third or fourth month, the effect of this micromanagement started to take its toll on the CEO. He saved many tactical decisions for these board meetings, asking the board to make the decisions. The meetings got even longer.

The VC partner who had introduced me to the company started confiding in me that David and the general were grossly undermining the CEO's authority and causing the CEO to be extremely tentative in decision-making. Other executives knew the CEO was being second-guessed in all of his decisions by the board and couldn't rely on what the CEO would tell them. The CEO called me to ask my advice about changing the behavior of David and the general at board meetings.

I advised the CEO to talk to the other board members to gain their support for approaching David and the general about their micromanagement behavior. The CEO was intimidated by David and the general and couldn't confront them directly. One of the directors talked to David and the general, and David told him all directors should behave like David. Apparently David and the general were not going to change their behavior.

After less than a year, the CEO resigned. Micromanagement by the two board members had made him feel like a chief operating officer rather than a chief executive. The company found another CEO who was content to assume the COO type of role.

About a year later, a large conglomerate acquired the company. The VC firms recovered their investment, but the common shareholders, including the founder and the option holders, received nothing.

The Board of Directors' Role

I've often seen CEOs invite a current or past chief executive of another company to become a board member, only to find out later that this person wants the board to micromanage the company. This comes as an unpleasant surprise for the CEO.

When several outside members of the board insist on micromanagement, the effects on the company can be severe. If members of the management team believe they'll be second-guessed by the board on minor, non-strategic decisions, the management team will be reluctant to make tactical or strategic decisions. In a young company, this can be devastating.

Although we usually think of the board of directors as having a fiduciary duty to the shareholders and the company, the practical role of the board is to provide oversight. Most commentators on corporate governance use the term oversight rather than fiduciary duty to describe the role of the board. However, the term oversight cannot be found anywhere in the statutes that govern the duties of a board of directors. Even the Sarbanes-Oxley Act of 2002, a federal law designed to curb corporate scandals like the Enron and WorldCom affairs, mentions oversight as part of a board's duties but does not define the term.

Does oversight include micromanagement? I'm afraid there's no bright line to show when oversight crosses into micromanagement. There's an old case decided by the U.S. Supreme Court in which the justice writing the opinion said of pornography, "I know it when I see it." I think any experienced businessperson knows micromanagement at the board level when he or she sees it.

I don't know any good CEO who can work effectively if several board members are in a micromanagement mode. I've seen CEOs burn out largely because the board spent almost all of its meeting time second-guessing minor decisions made or pending by the management team. For instance, I've seen board members in meetings argue with management over expenditures of $1,000 or less for what seems like hours when the monthly expenditures for the company exceed $1 million.

On the other hand, I've often observed boards whose outside directors were completely passive and said very little at board meetings. This is clearly the opposite of micromanagement and does not constitute oversight. In fact, it's seriously reckless conduct.

Handling Micromanagement

What can a CEO or other board member do when board members insist on micromanaging? If the CEO has the courage to address this at a full board meeting, he or she could ask for a resolution setting out in principle that the board will avoid micromanagement and focus on strategic issues and oversight matters. A resolution like this will put everyone on notice that a majority of the board does not want members to micromanage. However, in my experience, most CEOs are reluctant to directly address this issue with the board.

CEOs who don't feel they can address this issue head-on should find a board member willing to join them in taking the micromanaging board member aside to discuss the problem. If the micromanaging board member represents a large investor in the company, such as a venture capital firm, it can be very difficult to change this person's behavior. The CEO might have to choose whether to tolerate it or leave the company.

I've often recommended to CEOs working with a micromanaging board member to try to satisfy this person's needs by spending a significant amount of time with him or her before each board meeting, providing information and answering questions so the micromanaging doesn't occur during the board meetings. This sometimes works, but other times it backfires and provides the offending board member with more ammunition to try to micromanage at the meetings.

Effective Directors

During all of my 30-plus years of dealing with boards of directors, I've never met a board member who attended a seminar on being an effective director. I typically provide new directors with several publications on the subject, but there's no substitute for the education a seminar can provide.

An enlightened board would require all members, including those who are on the management team, to attend programs about being an effective director and would make it compulsory that the board perform a self-evaluation each year. The National Association of Corporate Directors has been encouraging this for years.

Partners in venture capital firms serve on many boards. Yet, I haven't met a single venture capitalist who has attended a program on being an effective director. I know their response to this criticism would be that they've learned how to be good directors by sitting on boards with experienced CEOs of other companies. This simply does not provide a thorough enough education about how to work with the CEO and focus on strategic matters, which is the path to avoiding micromanagement by the board.

13

Failing to Focus On Strategic Opportunities

or

"If we don't chase every opportunity, we might miss an important one."

Several years ago, I was asked by a venture capitalist friend to go with him on a visit to a company in Melbourne, Florida. He was considering investing in it and had advised the company to engage me as counsel because its current lawyer was not experienced at venture capital transactions.

The investor and I met with the company's founder, Doug, and heard a fascinating story. Doug was a student at the local university. He had been an enlisted man in the Marines for eight years and decided to get a pre-med degree with hopes of going to medical school. While attending classes, he worked part-time for a veterinarian who primarily treated dogs and cats. In the course of his studies, through research for a paper for one of his classes, Doug became fascinated with the painful side effects of chemotherapy used to treat children who had cancer.

He was a voracious reader and began studying the medical literature about possible treatments for cancer. He stumbled onto several research papers from the 1930s and '40s about a protein found in the wall of a bacterium that seemed to have the effect of stimulating the immune system to attack and kill tumors. Using the laboratory of the veterinarian at night, he was able to isolate this protein and find a way to harvest it in quantity from these bacteria.

With the help of the veterinarian, he injected cancerous tumors in several dogs that were terminally ill. The tumors contained different concentrations of this protein. According to the veterinarian, the tumors in some of the dogs shrank and, occasionally, disappeared. Of course, this seemed too good to be true. Doug and the veterinarian believed the protein "switched on" the dog's immune system, which then attacked the tumor. Doug and the veterinarian also injected this protein into several cats with feline leukemia and found that the cats recovered. Feline leukemia was usually fatal. Although the exact cause of feline leukemia was not known then, a virus was suspected.

Doug approached several potential investors to raise capital for well-controlled trials to determine whether the anecdotal results could be confirmed. The venture capitalist who introduced me to Doug wanted to invest. I agreed to serve as counsel for Doug's company and prepared a private offering memorandum to use with angel investors to raise about $1 million. The company raised the money and hired several PhDs, including one who had been with the U.S. Food and Drug Administration, where he was responsible for overseeing the approval of new drugs.

With the advice of several consultants, Doug decided to first produce a form of treatment for feline leukemia using the protein he had used in the laboratory of the veterinarian. At that time, therapeutic drugs for animals had to be approved by the U.S. Department of Agriculture, not the FDA. Doug believed he could gain USDA approval in short order and the data developed for that agency eventually would help the company in gaining approval from the FDA for using the protein for human treatment.

The company needed more capital, and the current investors – classic angel investors – kicked in another $2 million. With that money, Doug launched a program to gain USDA approval for the feline leukemia treatment, prepared a business plan to raise more capital, this time from venture capital firms, and hired several more PhDs.

I remember attending a meeting in Doug's conference room where he listed about 15 different research programs based on the protein he wanted to launch with new capital. This list would be the basis for a new business plan he intended to prepare for the venture capital firms. I was appalled at the lack of focus and told him so. He believed he could have his scientific staff work on all of these projects simultaneously. Worse, his board of directors agreed with him. None of the board members had ever been involved in a company with such high growth potential, so the directors thought this type of strategy was needed to appeal to the venture capital firms.

After preparing the new business plan, Doug launched most of the projects, increasing the monthly cash burn rate significantly. The first reaction to his business plan by several venture capital firms was a polite "no."

However, one firm in New York City told him it had an interest, but only if a consulting firm recognized in the therapeutic drug industry confirmed the technology and the company's strategy.

As with most development-stage companies, this one was rapidly running out of cash. Doug and I visited the consulting firm in New York and engaged it to do a report on the company. We offered the firm a significant cash incentive if the report could be completed in a short period of time. The consulting firm agreed. In three weeks, Doug and I were back in New York meeting with the consultants and the venture capital firm. The consulting firm issued a short report concluding that the technology had merit but the company needed to focus on one or two products, not the 15 proposed in the business plan.

The venture capital firm was impressed and agreed to form a syndicate with several other venture capital firms to invest about $8 million. One condition was that the company had to agree to hire an experienced executive as the CEO. The board of directors was expanded and now included two representatives of the venture capital firms.

At the first meeting of the new board after the closing, Doug made a presentation on the status of each of the 15 projects. I was at the board meeting as usual, and I was alarmed. How could Doug continue with the 15 projects when this was one of the major criticisms of his company by the consulting firm? Further, how could the two VC directors not call him to task for this? I learned after the meeting that Doug had convinced the VC directors he and the new CEO could manage all of these projects and there was no need to focus on only two. Why the VC directors accepted this logic, I'll never know.

Soon, the burn rate was nearly $1 million per month and the feline leukemia project was seriously behind schedule. Only two scientists on the staff were working on it. About 10 other scientists were assigned to different projects.

The new CEO had no experience in dealing with an entrepreneur. He had worked at two large pharmaceutical companies where entrepreneurial activities were discouraged. He found he could not convince Doug by using logic that the company needed to focus. Doug was brilliant and the CEO was no match for him in a logic contest. The CEO quickly gave up, thinking the VC directors must know better. Since the VC directors were not coming down hard on Doug to focus, he believed the VCs would support Doug in all the projects and not let the company run out of capital.

Unfortunately, the clinical studies the company submitted to the USDA in support of the feline leukemia treatment were seriously flawed. When one of the PhDs working on the feline leukemia project discovered the flaw, the company's consultant and special counsel advised the company that it had to immediately notify the USDA and withdraw the studies. The company's primary project would fail. The company had spent substantially all the capital it had raised, mostly on other, longer-term projects, and would run out of capital in a few months.

The CEO quit. The venture capital investors announced they would not provide more capital. Doug was asked to resign and the chief financial officer was asked to take over management of the company. The CFO slashed the payroll, reducing the number of employees from about 30 to four or five. One of the smaller venture capital firms that had invested provided a small amount of capital to keep the company alive while it gained USDA approval for the use of the protein in a treatment for a skin disease that affected dogs.

This treatment ultimately was approved and the company was acquired by a veterinarian supply company for about $1 million. No further effort was made to explore the use of the protein for other animal or human diseases. More than $15 million of investors' money was lost.

Why Companies Choose Unfocused Strategies

Everybody reads about focus, focus, focus. Every entrepreneur I've ever dealt with has quoted this to me and has said he or she possesses laser-like focus. However, the reality is that most entrepreneurs are not even capable of focusing.

I remember serving on a board of directors with Professor Howard Stevenson of Harvard University. Each board meeting was a classroom-like experience, with Dr. Stevenson providing an interesting lecture on a different topic. We enjoyed listening to him as he would tell us about the conceptual nature of various aspects of development-stage companies.

One time at dinner, Dr. Stevenson said that in his observation, entrepreneurs are driven by the opportunities they perceive. Entrepreneurs believe they can gather the resources to take advantage of an opportunity while they're in hot pursuit of that opportunity. In other words, entrepreneurs are willing to run full speed ahead toward the edge of a cliff, believing they'll raise capital or gather resources in some other manner before running off the edge.

On the other hand, the availability of resources drives conservative managers such as institutional trustees of a trust. These managers won't take the first step until all resources are in place that they believe are necessary for taking advantage of an opportunity. I've never seen a successful entrepreneur behave as a conservative manager. On the other hand, I've seen many entrepreneurs driven by opportunity who fail to raise enough capital and run off the edge of the cliff.

Every entrepreneur I've ever worked with was easily distracted by perceived new opportunities. Entrepreneurs will bounce from opportunity to opportunity without focusing on the primary one. The only successful way I've found to keep entrepreneurs from doing this is for investors to come down hard on them, requiring them to focus on the primary opportunity and put the others on hold. Entrepreneurs can seldom be convinced they should totally give up on an opportunity, but they can sometimes be persuaded to put the opportunity in a standby mode. Investors hope that when the primary opportunity has been fully addressed, the entrepreneur will have given up on those opportunities that are on standby.

Entrepreneurs feel so strongly about their own instincts, I've often seen them promise investors they'll focus on the primary opportunity and then continue to work on other opportunities, disguising their efforts as some activity related to the primary strategy. Too often, investors don't realize this is happening until the company is nearly out of cash.

Whether a company is large or small, the CEO must always keep it and its executive officers focused. I tell new CEOs their primary job is to say "no." And they must say "no" gently, so as not to make employees reluctant to bring new ideas and new opportunities to them. It's hard for lower-ranking employees to appreciate the need to focus on the company's primary opportunities. Management turns off these workers when it turns down their ideas without providing a believable explanation.

CEOs must stimulate all the officers reporting to them to be on the lookout for opportunities and to be creative but to accept rejection by the CEO and still come back with new ideas and opportunities. This is difficult for companies of any size.

If the CEO doesn't lead the company to focus, the company will surely fail as soon as the market for its products becomes highly competitive and the growth rate levels off. At this point, the company's resources will be inadequate to develop new products if those resources were consumed in chasing too many opportunities. Sun Tzu's book *The Art of War,* which is often quoted in discussions about focus, says an attacking force should concentrate on a single point. It shouldn't make a frontal attack unless the attacking force greatly outnumbers the defending force. By definition, development-stage companies don't have overwhelming force versus their large competitors. Therefore, all their resources should be focused on a single point of attack. It's the CEO's job to make sure resources aren't wasted on marginal opportunities that would increase the risk of failure with the primary opportunity.

How Entrepreneurs Can Learn to Focus

Most entrepreneurs cannot be taught to focus. They simply can't accept the need to do it, even though they promise to stay focused. It usually takes outside forces to cause the entrepreneur to choose to focus, such as investors refusing to provide additional financing unless the company agrees not to pursue marginal opportunities. Because entrepreneurs are driven by opportunity and not by the availability of resources, is it any wonder most of them can't take a task to its completion?

People willing to take the kinds of risks entrepreneurs take are those who can't perform the last 5 percent of any given project. They lose interest well before the project is 95 percent complete and are off looking at other opportunities. The first professional manager a development-stage company usually hires is a chief operating officer. That person is expected to have the opposite trait of the entrepreneur and will make sure all projects are 100 percent completed. However, this trait usually annoys company founders to no end. They see COO types as not sharing the grandiose vision the founders have for the company.

When company founders bring in, or are forced by the investors to bring in, a professional manager as a CEO, the founders invariably complain that the professional manager is not as driven by opportunities as are the founders. My response to this is that the founders are absolutely correct. However, I explain that the professional manager complements the entrepreneur because the manager will do those things the entrepreneur can't stand to do – including following each project to completion.

The CEO's Role in Maintaining Focus

Why is it that most CEOs can't succinctly state the company's business strategy even though it's clear the company has one? I wish I knew the answer to this question. As evidence that even large companies suffer from this, look at the money spent with consulting firms that often are tasked to develop a coherent and clear statement of strategy for a company. It should not take consultants to create a business strategy for a development-stage company. A consultant can gather information and recommend strategies, but the CEO must be capable of evaluating the information and developing the strategy. CEOs who don't have these skills should be replaced.

Consultants can be helpful in providing a conceptual framework for the business strategy and obtaining information about the market and competition. Based on this information, the CEO can develop a concise statement of the company's strategy. Other executives can and should have input into developing the strategy, but the CEO alone must make sure the strategy makes sense and is stated in clear terms. I often see statements posted throughout a company's offices that outline the company's strategy in broad language such as: "Our strategy is to provide the highest-quality products to our customers at the lowest, yet profitable price to our customers." This is total nonsense. This kind of statement is useless to the organization as a guiding statement. Consider this alternative: "After the large semiconductor manufacturers develop the market for memory chips, we will follow behind them to offer the gaming customer segment a superior product by customizing memory chips for higher performance using the company's proprietary design software." At least this statement of strategy would be a good start.

Of all of the companies I've represented, I can recall only two that would devote half of the time at each regularly held board meeting to a discussion of strategic matters. Each was successful in large part because of the clarity of its strategy to all employees who could have an impact on the company's performance. A clearly stated strategy will help the company take advantage of opportunities in good times and stay the course in bad times.

I'm convinced most CEOs and chief marketing officers don't know what it means to develop a clear, well-stated strategy. Many business books focus on the process of developing one, but only a few focus on the results and give good examples of strategy statements.

If a company develops a clear statement of its business strategy, each major function in the organization – such as human resources, operations or finance – can then develop its own strategy that's consistent with the overall plan and can help the company achieve its goals. But in my 30 years of experience, I can recall only one company that required the managers of each of its functional areas to prepare a strategy that would follow and implement the company's overall plan.

No matter how clearly the company's strategy is stated, department heads will need help in making the connection to create their own versions that contain as much thought and precision. Most people who head up these functions don't have the training or experience to think strategically. This is a clear dilemma for a CEO and for the board of directors. In most companies, functional heads are not hired for or promoted to the positions because of their strategic thinking. Often, a person who is a strategic thinker will not perform well as the head of a major functional element of the company because 95 percent of the job is related to tactical matters and not strategic issues.

One of the most important roles for a CEO is to make sure each function is performing under a strategy designed to be consistent with the company's overall focus. Put another way, a well-defined business strategy for the company acts as a filter for the CEO for all decisions to be made within any functional area of the company. It allows the CEO to say "no" often to things that are not consistent with the focus. If functional heads understand the company's strategy, they won't pester the CEO to do things that are inconsistent with it.

The Board's Role in Maintaining Focus

Almost all successful companies I've worked with did not succeed on the product or service that started the company. Once the company engaged the market and became fully aware of the competition's responses to its products, the company brought to bear all of its resources to focus on a new or modified product that led to success. The mission of a board of directors for a development-stage company is to make sure the company engages the market quickly, discovers the product that warrants its focus, and stays within the capital available to the company. I've seen many companies run out of cash just as they discover the niche they should pursue.

Most often, the board of directors of a development-stage company is controlled, directly or indirectly, by the entrepreneurial founders. Can we expect a board in this situation to persuade the CEO and the company as a whole to focus, focus, focus? The general answer is – no. However, if the founders have been smart enough to bring on several qualified outside directors, including one or more representatives of venture capital firms, then the outside directors should have the courage to make the founders realize the company is not focused. This is another one of those areas where companies can benefit from directors who are willing to ask hard questions.

I can remember attending a board meeting for a development-stage company that had raised a great deal of capital during the Internet craze. The CFO made a presentation about why the company should acquire another organization that was not in the mainstream business of the company. He said it could be the start of a new market for the company's products and services. Everyone seemed to be in favor of making this acquisition, and there was little discussion. I felt nervous about the company becoming defocused because the proposed acquisition would require a great deal of top management time at a crucial period in the company's development, when every second of the management team's time should be devoted to the company's primary business. I made this case. After some discussion, the board members agreed with me and the acquisition proposal was taken off the table.

Several days later, I was at a management team meeting for the same company and this proposal came up again for consideration. I jumped in and said I couldn't believe what I was hearing since the board of directors had made it clear the company should not be pursuing this acquisition. The members of the management team had been present at the same board meeting and had heard the same words I'd heard, as well as my reaction to the proposal made to the board. Members of the management team were inexperienced, and not a single one of them had ever been an executive officer of a company that acquired another organization. The management team members were caught up in the Internet environment, where capital was flowing so freely that financing to make an acquisition seemed to be readily available. Their basic argument for bringing up the acquisition proposal again was that they had the capital, the opportunity was there and, therefore, the company should make the acquisition. In other words, they believed the board of directors was wrong in turning down the proposed acquisition.

I had to make the same argument I'd made at the board of directors meeting. As if they were witnesses in a civil trial, I asked questions of several members of management about the amount of time they had available to devote to this acquisition. They clearly became uncomfortable in answering my questions since their answers supported my premise that they simply didn't have time to devote to an acquisition. They reluctantly agreed they shouldn't pursue this opportunity.

Ironically, within a few months, the company realized it was going to need more capital to penetrate its target market and learned the capital markets for Internet companies had closed. I remember saying to myself that the cash the company would have used to make the proposed acquisition was now extraordinarily valuable. The company had made the right decision in passing up the opportunity.

Periodically Reviewing the Company's Strategy

Boards of directors seldom review the basic strategy being followed by the company. This is as true for companies that are publicly held as it is for those in the development stage. Worse, most CEOs don't have a carefully considered strategy for their companies. How can the board of directors review a basic strategy that's vague or non-existent? One of the most valuable roles a board can play is to hold basic strategy review sessions at least twice a year – and more often for rapidly growing companies.

According to *The Art of War,* a strategic plan as well as a tactical plan must change as soon as the enemy is engaged. We can change this to apply to competitive markets by saying that as soon as customers are engaged and as soon as competitors react, the company's strategy and tactics must change to consider the competitive reaction and new information obtained directly from the marketplace.

What I find is that most companies adopt a business plan for the fiscal year that inherently states a business strategy if one digs deeply enough to find it. However, most business plans don't set out the business strategy in clear terms for everyone to understand. Further, most companies freeze the business plan for the fiscal year, thinking this is a way to discipline the company to make sure it doesn't change its budget just because there are changes in the marketplace, in competition, or in personnel. This is downright silly. Business strategy and tactics must be adapted as circumstances change.

Is it reasonable to expect a board of directors to review the basic strategy of the company often, such as every quarter? Are most members of the board capable of asking hard questions about the basic strategy of the company? This goes to the heart of selecting members of the board of directors.

My experience is that most members of boards of directors have no experience or expertise at strategic thinking. I know this goes against common wisdom, which says companies should select outside board members who are retired CEOs in related businesses or experienced investors. But

I've found these people don't necessarily have special expertise in strategic thinking.

Then why do I think the board of directors should review the basic strategy of the company often? One of the major roles of the board is to expect the company to develop a simple, straightforward statement of strategy that is compelling and makes common sense. In other words, the board can play much the same role as a trial jury. All trial lawyers know they must simplify the issues when presenting a case so the jury can focus on the big picture and not be mired down by insignificant details. This is what the board can do when reviewing the company's strategy, even if the board members have no special expertise at strategic thinking.

If the board of directors simply requires the CEO to review the basic strategy of the company at board meetings, the invisible hand of the board will have a significant effect on the CEO – who, in turn, will feel pressure to make sure the basic business strategy makes sense.

14

Not Recognizing the Company's Most Precious Resource is Management's Time

or

"I work a hundred hours a week at being CEO!
I don't have the time to think about strategy."

Susan started a software company to develop an Internet-based buying system for building contractors. She and a team of four programmers created a basic system and offered to let a few small homebuilders use it free of charge. She found several vendors who could offer products on the website. Then the company launched the site with primitive functionality.

Susan developed a business relationship with the chief operating officer of one of the largest homebuilders in Florida and convinced him her company could convert the primitive website into a tool that would serve the needs of his operation. The two companies entered into a complex contract to develop added functionality for the website. The contract called for periodic payments totaling more than $3 million.

Over the next several months, it became obvious the company couldn't possibly achieve the milestones in the contract within the time provided and that some essential elements of functionality could not be added. Instead of Susan throwing her efforts into finding solutions to the enormous problems developing with the company's large single customer, Susan spent time on other activities that only made the problem worse: trying to acquire other start-up companies, finding additional large customers by representing that the homebuilder's system was almost complete, seeking new customers outside the building industry to use the same system, and selecting which servers to use, such as Dell, IBM or off-brand names.

The homebuilder terminated its agreement with the company after about one year because the development was hopelessly behind schedule. Susan's focus on other matters had caused members of her management team to turn their attention to issues she should have been handling. As a result, the project had been managed inadequately. The company filed for reorganization under Chapter 11 but was unable to develop sustaining revenues and closed its doors. If only Susan and other members of her management team had devoted substantially all of their time toward their most important project, the company probably wouldn't have failed and lost more than $10 million for its investors.

Valuing Management's Time

Sooner or later, all development-stage companies become starved for cash. Even during the financial bubble of the 1990s, most companies that raised enormous amounts of money, either privately or through public offerings, burned through their capital before they could turn the corner and show positive cash flow.

The old saying "cash is king" always applies to development-stage companies. Many founders are so convinced capital is the most precious resource that they fail to place as much value on something even more important: the time of the founder and other members of the management team. One reason most companies end up cash-starved is because entrepreneurial founders chase after too many opportunities at the same time, as we discussed in **Chapter 13: Failing to Focus on Strategic Opportunities**.

Non-founding members of the management team in development-stage companies pick up on the attitude of the entrepreneurial founder and chase after too many opportunities within their functional areas. For instance, the person in charge of human resources and administrative functions often spends an enormous amount of time analyzing the terms of a proposed 401(k) plan when the company has 15 employees and doesn't intend to make matching contributions.

This is a waste of time for that person. The company should use the standard 401(k) plan recommended by one of the large financial institutions in its geographic area. There's no need to analyze all the bells and whistles for 401(k) plans at this stage of the company's development. The 401(k) plan can be modified sometime in the future, when the company has more than 100 employees. Too many companies get caught up in having a 401(k) plan designed to benefit top management when its primary function is to make the company competitive with other employers for non-management employees such as programmers and engineers. The HR person should be focused on more important things.

Another example is when the person in charge of purchasing items such as desktop computers or a network system obsesses over trying to find the highest performance for the lowest dollar. As a result, the company goes with a hodgepodge of suppliers to save money and ends up integrating the system itself. Inevitably, management spends an incredible amount of time solving problems and dealing with multiple vendors.

Hire the Experts

I advise development-stage companies to rely on the competitive nature of the market for all types of products such as desktop computers, telephone systems, health insurance, office furnishings and the like by going to a name-brand provider of these types of goods and services and not worrying about getting the lowest possible price. Efforts by a member of the management team in trying to find the lowest possible price for non-strategic goods and services is time and energy wasted.

As an example, a company that wants to buy desktop computers and have a network installed, even for 10 or 15 people, can go straight to IBM, Hewlett-Packard or Dell and have that one supplier take responsibility for doing it all. Yes, the out-of-pocket cash is likely to be 20 percent to 30 percent more than if the company bought the various elements of the network from different suppliers and used its own people to set up the network. However, the company is better served when management devotes its time instead to working with more potential customers to get feedback on the company's products or services. This reasoning is hard for founders of development-stage companies to accept when they're obsessing over managing cash flow.

The company can further offset that premium paid to brand-name suppliers by not buying unnecessary products and services. It makes more sense to buy only what the company needs right now in the form of desktop computers or network systems rather than buy a system with all kinds of bells and whistles that might be needed three years in the future. In development-stage companies, there often is an almost democratic decision-making process on these kinds of purchases, so the employee who makes the most noise tends to drive the specifications for these products or services, resulting in many added features that have little immediate value but add significantly to the cost.

Communicate the Company's Values

The CEO of a development-stage company must make sure every employee knows the difference between issues that are strategically important to the company versus routine or tactical matters. Every employee, from the receptionist on up, should be motivated to apply his or her time to the most valuable activity. It's easy for each employee's supervisor to provide a simple bullet-point list of the three to five activities to be performed by this worker that have the greatest value to the company. Employees should then try to use 80 percent of their time on those activities and 20 percent on other activities.

My observation is that most employees in development-stage companies do just the opposite. They spend 20 percent of their time on those things that are most valuable to the company and 80 percent on things that are less important strategically. This is especially true of the management team. The founder is usually the most guilty.

I draw a graph for founders of development-stage companies that shows on the horizontal axis the time scale for achieving the lofty vision of the founder, usually three to five years in the future. Then I add points on the time scale within the next six months when short-term milestones must be met in order to get to the lofty vision. Then I point out that usually the founder is spending 90 percent of his or her time and energy working on achieving the vision and only 10 percent on achieving near-term milestones. This is easy for company founders to do when they're driven by opportunity. As a result, it's hard for them to focus on the nitty-gritty and bring short-term projects to a conclusion. A better balance would be to spend 20 percent of the time on the vision and 80 percent on achieving near-term milestones. Unless those milestones are met, the vision can't be achieved.

When I show this chart to company founders, they invariably understand and agree with my observation. Yet, I have to remind them about this almost monthly and tell them which of their activities are wasted because they contribute very little to the company meeting the necessary near-term milestones. It's hard for entrepreneurs to quit dreaming about the future and focus on what must be achieved now. But they must so the company can stay alive long enough to raise capital for achieving the long-term goals.

15

Not Trusting Advisors

or

"Our corporate attorney advised us not to agree to the terms of the loan offered by the investors, but he's a lawyer, not a businessman."

Medfax, which distributed medical supplies for hospital emergency rooms and emergency-response paramedics, was a small publicly held company that had been struggling for years to remain profitable while it grew by offering new products. It had gone public more than 10 years earlier, when it was possible for small companies to have public offerings. The company's stock was traded on the bulletin board and often went several weeks without a single trade.

David, the company's president and founder, wanted to expand Medfax's business into selling medical supplies to entire hospitals as opposed to only emergency rooms. He also wanted to offer the company's own brand of certain supplies to develop a brand awareness for Medfax.

With the help of a local accounting firm that provided limited business planning services, David prepared a business plan based on expanding the company's product lines and developing its own brands. He decided he needed about $1.5 million, which would cover his marketing expenses, additional inventory, and the added accounts receivable Medfax would create.

David met with his commercial bank and was quickly turned down for a loan of this size. The bank was not willing to take a risk that the new business would produce enough cash flow to adequately cover the repayment of the loan.

Over the previous year, David had been contacted by several small investment banking firms that proposed to assist his company in selling convertible notes to foreign investors. This would be done under a provision in the federal securities laws that permitted companies to sell securities to foreign investors without going through the expensive process of filing a registration statement with the U.S. Securities and Exchange Commission.

Under this provision, the foreign investors were required to hold the stock for at least 60 days before reselling it in the open market in the United States. Many small publicly held companies were making these "Reg S" or Regulation S offerings, and trade magazines were touting them as a way for these businesses to raise capital inexpensively.

David received a term sheet from one of the investment bankers summarizing the Reg S offering. The terms provided that foreign investors would purchase convertible notes that would be due in 36 months and would carry interest-only payments until the due date. The notes had a floating convertible price. They could be converted by dividing the principal and accrued interest on them by the floating conversion price. The floating conversion price per share was determined by taking the average between the bid and the asked price for the five trading days before conversion and multiplying that figure by 0.85, which produced a 15 percent discount. There was no minimum conversion price, so theoretically, if the calculated conversion price went down to a few cents per share, the notes could be converted into a huge number of shares of common stock. At the time, the average between the bid and the asked price was about $1 per share.

The investment bankers assured David the foreign investors were "in for the long-haul" and that he shouldn't worry about the notes being converted if there was a temporary decline in the price of the stock.

David talked to one of the partners of his accounting firm, who advised him several of his firm's clients had conducted deals like this and that these companies were happy with the outcome.

At the time, David had a sole practitioner lawyer serving as outside counsel to the company who had limited experience with transactions like these. When his lawyer saw the term sheet, he felt uncomfortable and referred David to me. I met with David and went over the term sheet. I also reviewed the business plan about the new products and the company's strategy to brand certain products. I liked the business plan but hated the proposed terms for the sale of the convertible notes to foreign investors. I advised David that the SEC was scrutinizing the Reg S offerings because there were certain small investment bankers who were taking advantage of small companies like Medfax. I told him unscrupulous wealthy foreign investors often conducted their business in tax havens such as the Channel Islands.

David owned about 40 percent of the outstanding stock in Medfax, which gave him practical control over the company because the other 60 percent was held by many investors, none of whom owned more than 2 percent.

I asked David whether he could negotiate a minimum conversion price such as 75 cents per share to eliminate the possibility the notes could be converted into a large number of shares, causing David to lose control of the company. David told me the investment banker would not negotiate this provision, but that David was confident the stock price would rise rather than fall when the company announced its expansion plan. I told David unscrupulous investors could short the stock and drive the price down, then convert the notes at a low price. Because Medfax stock was so thinly traded, its price could be driven down with the sale of a small number of shares compared with the number of shares into which the convertible notes could be converted.

I advised David to contact other investment banking firms to see whether one of them would handle a private placement for the company on standard terms for investors in the United States. It was unwise to fund expansion of the business with debt because many things could go wrong or the expansion could be delayed. I advised him to raise equity dollars to carry out the expansion, not take on debt.

I also told him there are "pump and dump" artists who often pounce on small companies like Medfax, especially after a Reg S offering has been made. I repeatedly told David about the enormous danger in having the conversion price float with no minimum.

David should talk to several CEOs of small companies who had done Reg S offerings to get their views on the problems associated with them, I told him. He should also ask the investment banking firm for the names of several other companies that had used its services for Reg S offerings, and then he should talk to these companies. David assured me he would do these things over the next few days.

About one week later, David got back to me and said he'd decided to go forward with the Reg S offering on the terms proposed by the investment banking firm. He had talked to only one CEO of a company that had done a Reg S offering with the investment banking firm, and the CEO was satisfied with the results. I later found out that CEO had previously been a partner of one of the principals in the investment banking firm.

I again advised David to go slowly and to consider other alternatives, but he was eager to do this deal. I asked one of my younger partners to work with David to do all the legal work associated with the Reg S offering.

During the course of preparing the documents for the Reg S offering, my partner came to me with several matters that concerned her. She had proposed to the investment banking firm that each foreign investor agree in writing not to short the stock while holding convertible notes. The investment banker had refused to ask the foreign investors to sign the agreement. My partner also was concerned the investors might be U.S. residents who had formed entities in the tax havens and that these entities would be the investors. This would be a violation of Regulation S.

I agreed with her that the investment banker's refusal to ask the foreign investors to agree not to short the stock was a red flag. I also agreed we should get an opinion from a lawyer representing each of the prospective investors stating that the entity making the investment was not owned, directly or indirectly, by U.S. citizens.

My partner was eventually successful in adding a provision to the agreement, signed by the foreign investors, stating that purchasers of the convertible notes would not short the stock as long as the investor was holding convertible notes. My partner and I advised David that even though this provision was in the agreement, it would be difficult to find out whether any of the foreign investors shorted the stock. I also told David I would withdraw as counsel to the company after the offering because I didn't feel he was willing to listen to my advice.

The Reg S offering took place, and the company ended up with about $1.2 million after all fees and expenses were deducted from the proceeds. I withdrew as counsel, advising the board of directors that the company should engage another law firm. The company issued a press release about the success of the offering and the company's plans to expand its product lines and create its own brands. The stock price moved up slightly afterward.

About eight months later, the company had run into significant difficulties in getting manufacturers that would make some of the products under the brand name of Medfax. Further, several suppliers announced they wouldn't do business with the company if its sales branched out beyond emergency operations since a number of them sold products directly to hospitals for general use throughout the facilities.

When the company reported its results for the first nine months of the fiscal year, its stock price started to drop in light trading. Then the number of shares traded daily picked up significantly and the stock price began to drop rapidly. Within a few weeks, the bid price of the stock was 25 cents per share. The company received notices from almost all the foreign investors stating that they would convert their notes at a conversion price of about 22 cents per share. David was stunned. When it was over, the foreign investors held more shares in the company than David.

Within days after the convertible notes became common stock, David received a call from the investment banker saying a representative of the foreign investors wanted to meet with the company's board of directors. The meeting took place a few days later. The representative said the foreign investors would start a proxy fight to take control of the board of directors if the board didn't voluntarily agree to have several directors resign so the vacancies could be filled by people the foreign investors would appoint.

David was furious but knew he couldn't win a proxy fight. After much negotiation, David and the board agreed to the demands. Shortly afterward, the board fired David, agreeing to pay him the severance called for under his employment agreement. The foreign investors brought in a new CEO, and David remained as a member of the board of directors.

Initially, David was optimistic the foreign investors would arrange for added capital and cause the company to grow. However, within one year, the foreign investors had found a buyer for the company that paid slightly more than 50 cents per share for all of the outstanding stock. David received 50 cents per share for his stock also, but he probably could have sold his company 18 months earlier at $1 per share without doing the Reg S offering. The foreign investors made more than twice their money in less than 18 months after their initial investment.

Why Entrepreneurs Need Advisors

Entrepreneurs often make the mistake of failing to seek out advisors to help them in areas where they have no experience. Part of the entrepreneurial personality is to put on blinders that obscure the risks the entrepreneur is taking. If most entrepreneurs could see and understand these risks, they'd never get their ventures started. However, by having these blinders, entrepreneurs usually suffer from the "you don't know what you don't know" syndrome.

I chuckled when I saw a quote by U.S. Secretary of Defense Donald Rumsfeld before the Iraq war. He said, and I'm paraphrasing, "I don't worry about what we *know* we don't know; I worry about what we *don't know* we don't know." We suffer from not knowing what we don't know. We often see this in the form of belittling the role of others, or the work they perform, thinking their work is so easy that anybody could do it, whereas the work we perform is complex and difficult and that other people could not easily perform it.

I find this often in young companies, especially when CEOs with a technology background say accounting is simply a "bean-counting" function. I immediately know these CEOs don't know what they don't know because the accounting function is just as important as any other in the company.

How to Choose Advisors

Part of the "you don't know what you don't know" problem is that entrepreneurs don't know a qualified advisor from a non-qualified one. Having advisors who are knowledgeable in areas not well understood by the entrepreneur clearly is a way to protect against the problem. Yet, my observation is the entrepreneurial personality finds great difficulty in trusting advisors such as lawyers, accountants and management consultants. As a result, many entrepreneurs seek advisors based on their sense of personal chemistry with those people rather than experience level and qualifications. This is a serious mistake.

Most entrepreneurs never check references for advisors they're considering. Often, the founders of a company never even ask for references. Even if they do try to check, they're not skilled in asking the right questions and end up getting only glowing reports. When entrepreneurs let themselves be easily impressed by potential advisors' self-serving statements and engage those people based on immediate chemistry with them, it's a result of the impulsive personality characteristic of most business founders. However, entrepreneurs don't view their quick decision-making as impulsive; they see it as the ability to make quick decisions as opposed to management personnel they've known in the past who take forever to resolve issues.

Even when an entrepreneur engages a seemingly qualified advisor, he or she is reluctant to trust that person's advice because the advisor lacks knowledge about the entrepreneur's specific type of business. This happens because entrepreneurs ask for advice after giving the advisor only a superficial review of the matter, usually as a means of saving money. As a result, the advice is often too vague to be useful to the entrepreneur.

An entrepreneur is better off engaging consultants or advisors with direct experience in the entrepreneur's type of business. That makes it doubly hard to find qualified advisors. And those advisors undoubtedly will be more expensive.

Figure 1

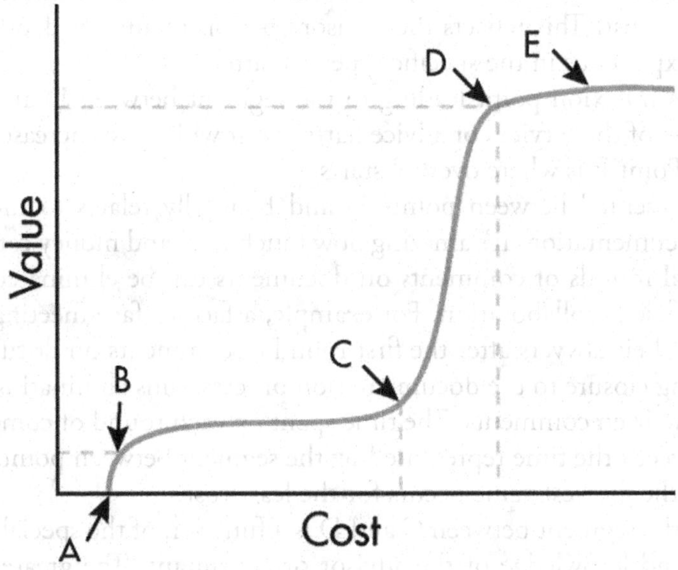

There's an S-curve that applies to cost versus the value of advice given or work performed by consultants and other service providers, including law firms. **Figure 1** identifies the different segments of that S-curve. The vertical axis is the value of the advice or services provided by the advisor or consultant, and the horizontal axis is the cost. The segment from the zero point to Point A shows there's an initial cost with no value while the consultant learns the basics of the assignment. The segment from A to B shows a quick rise in value for fairly little cost, but the value is still hardly significant. This represents the instant advice advisors give with only a superficial understanding of the matter after they've been engaged.

If the entrepreneur is willing to invest in a process that leads to higher value by allowing the advisor to spend more time on the matter, there will be a slow rise in value while the cost increases significantly as shown by the segment from B to C. There's a cost for the advisor to really dig into and understand the matter in the context of the business, the entrepreneur, the management team, and other factors. The more experience the advisor has with the type of business started by the entrepreneur, the shorter this segment becomes.

Point C shows a turning point in value, which occurs after the advisor has invested serious time in exploring the factors involved in the matter. The segment from C to D shows a rapid rise in value for a small, incremental increase in cost. This reflects the advisor's or consultant's in-depth knowledge and experience in the specific type of matter.

Point D is an inflexion point leading to the segment between D and E, where the value of the services or advice flattens out while cost increases rapidly. Beyond Point E is where overkill starts.

The cost represented between points D and E usually relates to the work done on documentation. It's amazing how much time and money can be saved if several rounds of comments on documents can be eliminated through more efficient collaboration. For example, a face-to-face meeting of all parties and their lawyers after the first round of comments on documents might bring closure to the documentation process, thus eliminating many rounds of written comments. The time spent on each round of comments usually exceeds the time represented by the segment between points C and D, where the greatest value occurs for the least cost.

The slope of the segment between C and D is a function of the specialized experience and knowledge of the advisor or consultant. The greater the specialization, the steeper the slope, meaning value is added quickly for only small increases in cost. If, on the other hand, the advisor or consultant doesn't have significant experience and knowledge and is, in effect, learning on the job, the slope of the segment from C to D will be less, meaning that value will increase at a slower rate per dollar than if the consultant has significant experience and knowledge.

What does all this have to do with entrepreneurs and selecting consultants or advisors? Smart entrepreneurs quickly realize they should insist the advisor work near Point D. Most entrepreneurs force consultants to work in the range of the segment from A to B by imposing cost limits on them without understanding how to identify the inflexion at Point C. This means the entrepreneur has to have the courage to allow the consultant to get to the inflexion, reach Point D and keep the segment between D and E as short as possible. The entrepreneur will have to pay the consultant more than originally expected, but the services will have substantially greater value.

I can put this in the context of services provided by a law firm. I usually tell our younger lawyers it's extraordinarily important to understand the client's business because this will shorten the segment from B to C of the S-curve. In other words, the lawyer can quickly get to the point where he or she is providing advice that considers the business context faced by the entrepreneurial company. I also point out that by specializing in a particular area, the slope of the segment from C to D will be steep and the value added to the client can be significant.

The more entrepreneurs understand this concept, the more quickly they can overcome their natural tendency to be paranoid, believing everyone is out to take advantage of them, including advisors. Since most advisors charge by the hour, the entrepreneur usually believes the advisor has an economic incentive to work many more hours than necessary. This, of course, can happen, especially when the consultant or advisor is working outside his or her area of knowledge or specialty.

How is the entrepreneur to know how much time the consultant or advisor should spend on an assignment? Frankly, the amount of time is largely controlled by the ethics of the consultant or advisor. One way to cause outside forces to control that variable is to hire a consultant or advisor who is very busy. This, of course, is a two-edged sword. Being that busy puts consultants under a great deal of pressure to spend only the amount of time on the assignment that they believe is necessary because they have many other demands on their time. On the other hand, busy advisors might devote only sporadic time to the project, taking longer than promised.

My experience is that an advisor or consultant whose references check out and who is very busy will devote the optimum amount of time to the assignment. He or she is too busy to overkill it.

Entrepreneurs who use a thorough process in selecting a consultant or advisor realize the difference in performance they receive for their money, convincing them of the true value of a qualified advisor. This leads to a trusting relationship.

16

Not Realizing How Quickly A Company Can Fail

or

"I know we'll run out of cash in exactly two months and 10 days, but I'm confident we can raise capital before then."

Bill started a business to make equipment that would help telephone companies test the capacity of their lines to transmit data at high rates. He had worked for a company that made communications equipment for the U.S. space program and had a great deal of experience in developing this kind of testing device. Bill learned quickly how to raise capital from angel investors and spent about 50 percent of his time on a continuous basis seeking money. He believed the value of his company increased over time and that selling too much stock at once would result in greater dilution of his holdings than if he sold smaller amounts every few months at a higher price per share each time.

Several of Bill's early investors who were on his board of directors were nervous about this approach to raising capital. Their fears became real when Bill hired several new engineers and launched an aggressive effort to complete development of the new product in three months. The company's monthly burn rate increased significantly, and the company had enough cash to operate for only another five months. Bill believed he could raise capital at a higher price per share once the new product was developed. The board members were worried Bill would not be able to raise capital before running out of cash.

The effort to develop the new product ran into significant difficulties, and it became clear the company wouldn't complete the work on time. Bill, knowing about the board's concerns, did not advise the directors of the delay. Instead, he began talking to new people about investing in the company, believing he could raise the necessary capital without having the new product completed. During the presentation, he told prospective investors of the new product under development. Each prospective investor told him to come back when the development was completed. When it became obvious the company would run out of money, Bill told his directors, expecting them and his other investors to come up with money.

However, he had waited too long. When his directors realized the extent of the crisis, and that he had not told them about the product development delay, they lost confidence in him. They told him they wouldn't make a further investment unless he found a new CEO. Unfortunately, they lacked experience as venture investors and didn't realize it would be impossible to find a new, qualified CEO in such a short period of time. Further, they discovered the company had strung out payments to its trade creditors, so several of them were about to sue for payment. The company had to file for protection from its creditors under Chapter 11 of the Bankruptcy Act. It never recovered.

When Financial Failure is Near

I've worked with many companies that saw financial failure looming because they were in negative cash flow with little prospect of raising more capital or getting significant new orders. Development-stage companies operate at a negative cash flow while they're developing their product and customer base. Predicting how long it will take to develop a meaningful revenue stream when introducing a new product is tough.

When companies operate at a negative cash flow, top management and the board of directors are usually optimistic about when revenues will start and how rapidly they'll ramp up. As cash begins to dwindle and revenues don't develop at the rate previously projected, board members start to become nervous. Ironically, company leaders become even more optimistic at this time that they'll be able to obtain new orders for the product or more financing for the company. When the situation continues with revenues not developing at a satisfactory level, and the company continuing to operate at a negative cash flow, most inexperienced board members shift from being worried to becoming optimistic because of the positive outlook of the management team.

The company finally reaches a point where management argues that no further cuts can be made in expenses because to do so will either weaken the company's ability to perform if it gets new customers or the cuts will be a sign of weakness in the eyes of potential investors. Every time I see a company cross this point, I know the end is near.

The management teams of most young companies, including those that are publicly held, have never been required to lay off employees. Even though more experienced people on the board of directors have been in situations that required layoffs, the management of these companies often resists addressing the need to reduce current expenses significantly. There's a psychological inertia built into a management team that has never experienced difficult economic times.

Revenues fail to develop as predicted because the adoption rate for the new product is usually much slower than predicted. A development-stage company has no control over the rate of acceptance of the company's product, especially if the product serves a new market or must displace existing competitive products. Of course, the company's founders have great expectations about how quickly the market will respond. The entrepreneurs believe they or their sales force can use aggressive selling tactics to cause customers to buy their products even when the customers must be "educated" about the benefits of them.

So what happens to a development-stage company when it's running out of cash and both the management team and the board of directors have entered a state of denial? It starts to grasp for low-probability opportunities such as a strategic partnership or acquisition by a publicly held shell company, or it engages an unknown "capital raiser" who promises access to many investors, including some that are offshore. Members of the board of directors, who should know better, usually don't speak up and are, along with the management team, "frozen at the stick."

There finally comes a time when the management team and the board realize the company is going to miss payroll or, if it has borrowed money from a bank, will default on the loan. Suddenly, the board of directors is interested in what it takes for the company to file a petition under Chapter 11 of the Bankruptcy Act. At this time, I'm usually asked to summarize the process of filing a Chapter 11 petition and operating under Chapter 11.

I always have to advise the board that the company will have to make a sizable payment to a bankruptcy law firm before filing the petition, with the amount based on the complexities of the matter because the bankruptcy law firm has no real assurances of being paid for a long time. Often the company is already so short of cash that it can't even muster the money to pay the bankruptcy law firm. Although most management teams claim this comes as a shock to them, invariably I can point to a prior meeting or a prior e-mail or some other form of communication where I or someone else advised them of the expenses involved just to file a Chapter 11 petition.

I also have to advise the board of directors that, typically, my law firm cannot serve as the one to take the company into a Chapter 11 proceeding because we are a significant creditor. Being a creditor, we will have a conflict with the company when it tries to reduce its creditor obligations under Chapter 11. This means the company will have to engage a lawyer who is a stranger in order to file the Chapter 11 petition and to operate under Chapter 11.

I also point out to the board the company must have enough resources to continue to operate under Chapter 11 either through a new cash infusion or through current revenues. The company will be excused temporarily from paying any of its unsecured accounts payable but must continue to pay expenses such as rent, payroll, payroll taxes and health care insurance. If the company has no means for continuing to make these payments with revenues it's receiving or a capital infusion, the company is facing liquidation.

A troubled development-stage company that has been financed by venture capital firms will sometimes be rescued by these firms. The current terminology for a rescue is a "restart," in which the current venture capital firms put in more money on terms that essentially wipe out the equity interests of the other shareholders. My observation is the venture capital firms will never come to the rescue of a company under these circumstances unless the CEO is replaced. Since the management team is in denial about what the company faces, it usually puts up great resistance to this proposition. However, almost overnight, as the outcome becomes unavoidable, the CEO and other members of management realize the company won't survive unless it gets a new chief executive.

It's understandable that an entrepreneur might freeze at the stick when faced with financial failure because that person probably has never been in this kind of situation before. It's not understandable that outside board members freeze at the stick. They should know the realities of impending financial failure. I've experienced this many times, and it always amazes me how my warnings and the warnings of others about the need to take immediate and aggressive steps to head off failure are disregarded.

17

Setting up the New CEO to Fail

or

"As the founder of this company, I agreed with the board that we should have an experienced businessperson like Susan as the new CEO. But she's been here for six months now and still doesn't understand our business."

Two engineers at a large defense company had helped develop a new material for printed circuit boards that had superior performance qualities to the material typically used. They learned the defense company had decided to abandon this technology because it was not of practical use in its business. Ron and Jack decided to start their own company and approached their employer about getting a license to the patents covering this material.

After several months of negotiation, they bought an exclusive license to the 12 patents that covered the new material as well as the process for making it. Ron and Jack started PC Materials Inc. and, over the course of a year, raised substantial capital, first from an angel investor group and then from a group of venture capital firms. They promised the venture capital firms they'd seek an experienced CEO since neither of them had experience running a company.

Ron and Jack were slow starting to find a new CEO. They found one only after considerable saber rattling by the venture capital firms. The founders assured the new CEO that customers would be willing to pay a price about 50 percent higher than the price of the material currently used because of the superior performance of the new material. Ron and Jack also assured the board of directors they'd fully support the new chief executive.

The CEO quickly determined large producers of PC boards wouldn't pay a higher price and wouldn't deal with a new company because of the risk it would go out of business once they had come to rely on it as the only supplier of the new material.

The CEO recommended to the board of directors that the company sublicense its new technology to PC board producers so these manufacturers could have the material produced in China at a cost significantly lower than the company's production cost. Ron and Jack disagreed, saying the profits to be made were in manufacturing the material, not in licensing the intellectual property protecting it. The board disagreed with Ron and Jack and encouraged the CEO to pursue the licensing strategy.

The CEO recommended that the number of employees at PC Materials be drastically reduced since the company would not be in the manufacturing business. Unknown to the CEO, the founders had organized a rebellion among the company's engineers and had mounted a secret campaign to discredit the CEO in the eyes of each director. A special board meeting was scheduled to deal with the layoffs.

As the CEO prepared to make his presentation at the meeting, the chairman – a partner in one of the venture capital firms that had invested in the company – announced the CEO would be terminated along with several members of his staff and that the company would go back to the strategy of making the new material, not granting licenses to it. The chairman advised the other board members that each of the key engineers said he would resign if the CEO continued as head of the company and that the board could not take the risk that they'd leave. The CEO was caught by surprise, but Ron and Jack were ecstatic. Jack was appointed chief executive officer.

A few months later, the chairman, Ron and several of the engineers went on a "road trip" to visit potential customers. About halfway through the trip, the chairman called the board members to report that every potential customer they visited told them, in no uncertain terms, that their organizations would only consider licensing the new material and would not buy the material from the company. The chairman realized the CEO had been correct and that Ron and Jack had used the other directors to get rid of him.

The venture capital firms took over the company and tried to sell it. With no buyers coming forth, the company was reduced in size to two employees whose job it was to answer inquiries about sublicensing the patents licensed by the company from the defense company.

Hiring Professional Management

Many times during my career, I've seen companies outgrow their founder or founders from a management standpoint, and the board of directors usually has the wisdom to persuade the founders to bring in professional management. This most often occurs with companies that have been funded by venture capital firms. The directors appointed by the venture capital firms usually have been through this before and there's an understanding with the founders that the venture capital firm expects the founders to find a qualified CEO in the near future. This transition is always difficult for the founders.

As I think back on 30 years of dealing with this, I believe that in more than half of the cases, the founders sabotaged the CEO so the executive could not be effective. The result is the new CEO either quits or is terminated by the board.

Let me walk you through the typical transition that takes place. A technology company is founded by one or more people who appoint themselves to the top management positions in the company and make it through the early development stage. A product or service is developed, revenues begin to come in, and the company is on a high-growth path. The company is not profitable at this time, but revenue projections show it will be very profitable in the future. The company has been funded by one or more venture capital firms, but the founders, together, still hold controlling interest in the company, although the venture capital firms have veto power over major corporate actions.

The founders are aware of the prevailing wisdom that it takes a very different person to found a company and take it through the development stage than the person who can manage the company once it's reached a certain level of revenues. Company founders always tell me they recognize this will occur and that they'll be glad to step aside when it's necessary. Yet, as the company becomes more and more dysfunctional and revenues begin to increase, the venture capital firm representatives on the board of directors become increasingly vocal about the need to bring in a professional CEO and CFO. The founders begin to have serious second thoughts about wanting to make the transition to a professionally managed company.

Finding Qualified Candidates

At some point, the venture capital directors persuade the founders to hire an executive placement firm to find a qualified CEO and, perhaps at the same time, a qualified CFO. The founders complain loudly that an executive placement firm is too expensive and will be ineffective. The founders suggest one or two candidates who are friends of theirs. The venture capital investors insist on taking a professional approach and, over the objections of the founders, engage the executive placement firm.

When candidates for the CEO position are identified and interviewed, the founders consciously or subconsciously start their sabotage campaign before the new CEO is even selected. The founders make it known to interviewees that a new CEO will have to consult them before making any significant proposal to the venture capital directors. Most interviewees are non-committal about this or agree, saying they'll do this out of respect for the founders. This conversation usually is not disclosed to the venture capital directors.

Most founders feel seriously threatened by a qualified candidate for the CEO position because they've never worked directly with a qualified CEO. If they came from a large technology company, they probably didn't report directly to the CEO. If they came from another small technology company, it's likely the CEO was still the founder and not a professional manager. It becomes another one of those situations where "you don't know what you don't know." The founders simply don't know what the qualified CEO candidate knows about management, strategy, financial matters and even the state of the competitive technology.

Founders will campaign for a non-threatening CEO. All venture capital directors know these dynamics are taking place. Tension exists throughout the process because the venture capital directors want to bring in a qualified CEO while the founders want to bring in a mediocre CEO. If the founders still control the company, the founders will prevail even though the venture capital directors are unhappy about the candidate who's selected. The venture capital directors will often have the view that a less-than-qualified candidate is better than continuing with one of the founders as the CEO.

On the other hand, the venture capital directors have leverage over the company, and the founders, when the company needs more capital. The venture capital directors make it clear they won't support the new round of financing unless a professional CEO is brought in. In this type of "cram-down," it's obvious the founders will be unhappy. They'll try to sabotage the new CEO in every respect. Venture capital directors are familiar with this problem and try to help the new CEO establish relationships with lower-ranking employees immediately so the employees' loyalty transitions to the new CEO. The founders try their hardest to keep the employees loyal to them instead.

Too often, I've seen boards of directors face a difficult choice: Should the new CEO be terminated even though he or she is highly qualified, or should several lower-ranking employees or, if possible, the founders, be let go so the CEO can do the job? Most of the time the CEO is terminated on the belief that the lower-ranking employees – for instance, the key technical people in a technology company – are so important that the company can't afford to lose them if they're threatening to leave unless the CEO goes.

The CEO usually has an employment agreement with a severance provision and the company has to pay the severance required. Then the board has to again launch the process of finding a new CEO. Usually the company remains in great turmoil for many months after this occurs.

Why CEOs Are Set Up to Fail

I attribute this behavior by founders to a common trait of entrepreneurs: They think everyone is out to take advantage of them. Why do company founders act this way? I've had to counsel many founders going through this process. Almost all founders say the new CEO doesn't understand the company, doesn't understand the technology and is trying to set up controls over the entire organization that will stifle creativity. The founders lack appreciation for the skills the CEO brings to the company that are necessary for growth and profitability.

In looking back over my career, I can recall only two times when the founder of the company supported the selection of a highly qualified new CEO and helped that person become effective. Both of these companies were highly successful.

Unfortunately, most outside directors on the boards of development-stage companies – unless they're partners in venture capital firms – have little experience in dealing with entrepreneurs and little experience, if any, in dealing with this situation. The founders often co-op the outside directors in their efforts to sabotage a new CEO. Unwittingly, the outside directors, other than those from VC firms, often are convinced by the founder that the new CEO has to go. The outside directors often become the key to whether a new CEO will be allowed to be effective.

The Role of Directors

How should outside directors deal with founders knowing they usually want to sabotage a new CEO? Usually the founder is moved into a position such as chairman of the board with no further executive authority, or to a job such as chief scientist or chief technology officer with no staff support. Sometimes the founder remains as CEO and the new executive is brought in as chief operating officer or COO, but the board views the new executive as the true head of the company. Making the new professional manager the COO, with the view that over time the COO will become the CEO, is seldom effective.

A new compensation scheme might induce the founder to be cooperative. In almost all cases when company founders are moved out of the CEO position, they suddenly feel they should be treated as key employees with stock options and other forms of compensation that have not been available them because founders have large stock holdings. Frankly, if this compensation helps in the transition, the board should grant the founder a stock option and create a bonus plan based on performance. The goal is not to capture the creative energy of the founder, but to induce the founder not to interfere with the new CEO.

18

Not Understanding The Acquisition Process

or

"I have a friend who knows the CEO of National Electronics, and he assures me his company wants to acquire us and close in 20 days."

Charlie and Tim worked for a large defense contractor in the field of satellite imaging. Most of their work was classified because of the sensitive nature of spy satellites. However, they had worked with several others in the company to develop computer software that could be used to "stitch" photos together to create one image of a large geographic area. Charlie and Tim recognized there could be commercial applications for this software if it was used with aerial photography.

They approached their company about this opportunity. The company didn't want to get into the commercial market for this activity but agreed to license certain parts of the software to a new company started by Charlie and Tim.

After setting up their business, Charlie and Tim launched an effort to convert the software for use with commercial aerial photography. They envisioned their customers would include land developers, large farming operations, oil exploration companies, mapping companies, state and local governments, and other operations that use aerial photographs.

One problem they had to overcome is that distortions occur when several photographs are stitched together to show large geographic areas. Charlie and Tim knew they could modify the software to eliminate almost all of the distortion. The project looked promising, and Charlie and Tim raised about $1 million from local investors. The money was used primarily for developing the software. After a few months, the company approached several venture capital firms and was successful in raising $3 million from three of them, which was expected to take the operation to a break-even point. A substantial part of the $3 million would be used to develop a marketing organization and to initiate contacts with aerial photographers and users of aerial photography.

As often happens with new technology, the potential customers had to be convinced of its value. Charlie and Tim had to show potential customers how they could use distortion-free photographs stitched together to make an image of a large geographic area. However, aerial photographers were reluctant to offer this service to their clients because of the added expense.

Revenues grew slowly, and it became obvious the company wouldn't reach a break-even point before running out of the $3 million capital infusion. The venture capital firms pressured Charlie and Tim to find a buyer for the company because they were unwilling to invest more money.

Charlie and Tim didn't like the idea of selling, so they began looking for other sources of capital. They met with several "finders" who said they could raise capital for the company from unusual sources such as wealthy families in the Middle East, investors in various tax havens that would guarantee bank loans, and even real estate investors who were used to putting money into tangible assets but not intangible services. Charlie and Tim spent most of their time running down each of these possibilities despite my warnings that none of these sources was credible and despite the genuine concern of the venture capital firms that they were wasting time they could be devoting to finding someone to acquire the company.

As the date when the company would run out of cash came closer, Charlie and Tim became more and more disconnected from the reality of the situation they faced. They contacted several large companies in an effort to find an acquirer, but quickly learned that large companies were not interested in making such a small acquisition. Finally, a friend told Charlie about an oil exploration company in California interested in acquiring the company. Charlie's friend told him a vice president there had assured him the oil exploration company could perform its due diligence on Charlie and Tim's company and close an acquisition within a matter of three or four weeks.

The company had sufficient cash to last about two months before it would go under. Charlie and Tim announced to the board of directors that they could strike a deal, negotiate the definitive agreements and pull off the acquisition within four weeks, leaving a cushion of four weeks of operating cash. Several board members and I told Charlie and Tim they were crazy to believe they could negotiate and close the deal in less than 90 days. We suggested the company drastically cut its monthly expenses to buy more time.

Charlie and Tim argued that if they cut back now, the oil exploration company would see this as weakness and would demand a much better deal for itself or would not want to do the acquisition because of the software company's reduced capability. They refused to make the cutbacks.

Unfortunately, after about six weeks, it became painfully clear the oil exploration company wanted to do a great deal of due diligence and had no intention of speeding up the acquisition. As it turned out, Charlie's friend had talked to the vice president of international operations for the oil exploration company, who had nothing to do with acquisitions.

Although Charlie and Tim were successful in negotiating a term sheet for the acquisition, they ran out of money before they could negotiate a definitive, binding agreement with the oil exploration company. Charlie and Tim's company had to file for reorganization under Chapter 11. The employees left, and the software license from the defense company terminated because Charlie and Tim's company was unable to pay the minimum royalties. Seeing these signs, the oil exploration company backed off.

The company went out of business and the investors, as well as Charlie and Tim, lost their entire investment.

Understanding the Acquisition Process

All companies financed by venture capital firms have a clearly stated exit plan of either being acquired or going public. Given the dramatic changes in the stock market over the past several years, going public isn't as common an option. So the eventual fate of most development-stage companies and many small-cap publicly held companies is to be acquired. Development-stage companies are also acquired when they hit a wall in raising capital and need a way out.

What goes on at the board level when a company considers being acquired? Every deal has different dynamics, but there are common threads in each acquisition. Because of the nature of my practice with young technology companies, almost all of my experience in acquisitions has been in connection with representing the target company – that is, the company being acquired.

There are times when a private company engages an investment banker and seeks out an acquisition on a well-planned basis even if the company isn't in financial trouble. When a company has the luxury of making this type of decision, the process is much less tense, but the CEO and the directors should still understand what they face during the acquisition process to ensure a smooth transaction.

When a company realizes it must seek an acquirer because it's running out of capital, there's usually a short fuse. As soon as the company receives a serious proposal from an acquirer, board members realize they must do everything possible to make the acquisition happen.

Different Stages of Financing

Let's follow the route of a company realizing it must be acquired because it can't raise capital to continue. Often a company raises just enough money from angel investors for the company to produce a prototype of its products and then seeks venture capital money to take the company to the revenue-producing stage.

Today, there's an overreaction to the financial bubble, and venture capital firms are being extraordinarily cautious. As a result, the first round of funding from venture capital firms must be of a size to take the company to the revenue-producing stage. The risk of being able to raise additional capital after the prototype stage but before the company produces revenue is too great in the eyes of venture capital firms. They won't invest in development-stage companies that will need two rounds of financing before producing revenue.

It's very difficult today to raise capital in a Series A round for more than $5 million from venture capital firms, There are still cases that involve tens of millions of dollars in the first round of financing, but these are unusual.

Applying the current rules of thumb, most venture capital firms that are investing in Series A rounds put their money only in companies that need $5 million or less to get to the revenue-producing stage. If the company is a pure start-up, then the $5 million must take it all the way through to that point. Most venture capital firms today won't invest in a company just to take it to the prototype stage. This means an early stage company must raise capital from angel investors to get started.

When a company raises only $5 million or less, there's a high probability it won't reach the revenue-producing stage before running out of capital. This means more companies that receive Series A funding from venture capital firms will need to be acquired before they produce significant revenues. Further, most companies funded by angel investors that can't get beyond the prototype stage must be acquired.

When Acquisition Becomes Necessary

So let me discuss the dynamics that go on when a company decides it needs to be acquired because it's running out of capital. In almost every instance, a company in this situation tries to raise capital at the same time it's attempting to be acquired. One reason for this is to give potential acquirers the perception the company has the alternative of raising capital versus being acquired. When a company launches an effort to be acquired, it always wants to develop a perception of competition among potential acquirers or a perception the company doesn't need to be acquired. In my experience, companies seldom have two or more potential acquirers expressing a strong interest at the same time. Therefore, the perception of competition has to be developed in other ways.

One way is to demonstrate to potential acquirers the company is in the process of raising capital from venture capital firms or from strategic partners. Another way is for the company to engage a reputable investment banking firm to seek potential acquirers, if the company is big enough to appeal to investment banking firms. Having a reputable firm seeking potential acquirers gives the sense that other potential buyers will be found.

The company usually prepares a business plan or similar document to provide to potential acquirers. If the company is not large enough to use an investment banker, the company does this on its own through contacts usually provided by its venture capital investors. Of course, one of the primary targets will be the company's principal competitor.

The CEO and CFO of the company suddenly become consumed in this process, usually to the detriment of any ongoing capital-raising effort. Most of the time, the directors who aren't the representatives of venture capital investors are passive in this effort and become involved only when there are serious discussions taking place between the company and a potential acquirer. The venture capital investors might provide bridge financing between the time the company makes the decision to be acquired and the time of the acquisition as a means of protecting their investment. Of course, potential acquirers quickly learn that bridge financing has been provided and realize the target company has little bargaining power.

My observation is the CEO of the target company in every case becomes convinced he or she can find a strategic buyer for the company rather than a financial buyer. A strategic buyer is one that wants to be in the company's business or wants to acquire its technology because those actions would align with the buyer's strategic path. Competitors are not usually strategic buyers unless the company owns some type of unique, proprietary technology. Otherwise, a competitor simply looks at the company as added capacity for a product line the competitor probably already offers – and competitors generally are not willing to pay a premium for added capacity.

Financial buyers are financial groups or are often corporate conglomerates that will buy almost any company when the terms are right. Under the circumstances, it's not likely a private financial group will buy the company if the venture capital firms won't provide financing to it.

Understanding the Decision Process

Most of the time the CEO has never been through an acquisition and is easily misled by statements a potential acquirer makes about its degree of interest. Further, the CEO doesn't understand the decision-making process that goes on in a potential acquirer's office and usually believes an acquisition can take place in a short period of time. Likewise, the CFO often has never participated in an acquisition and is as naïve about it as the CEO.

Also, the board members who aren't involved with the venture capital firms have little or no experience at acquisitions themselves and are of little use to the CEO in this process. Further, the CEO, by this time, is usually at odds with the board members from the venture capital firms and doesn't believe anything they say. As a practical matter, the CEO is left without qualified advisors unless outside counsel to the company has substantial experience and can advise the CEO about the realities of the process.

Handling the Paperwork

As soon as a prospective acquirer takes an interest, the two companies sign a mutual non-disclosure agreement and the acquirer begins its due diligence effort. Most of the time, the acquiring company does superficial due diligence initially and makes a proposal to the company in the form of a term sheet that outlines proposed terms of the deal – such as whether it involves cash, stock, notes or a combination of these – along with the proposed valuation of the deal and details about other issues important to the potential acquirer. The CEO takes this term sheet to his or her board for authorization to negotiate definitive agreements and to provide substantial additional information about the company to the potential acquirer.

Sometimes the potential acquirer and the company enter into a nonbinding letter of intent. However, publicly held companies are less likely to use these for fear they'll have to publicly disclose they're negotiating an acquisition.

A thorough due diligence study follows, managed by the lawyers for the potential acquirer, although the accounting firm for the acquirer might also become heavily involved in reviewing the target company's books and records. The primary objective of the due diligence study is to make sure everything the target company has disclosed is true. A secondary objective is to discover problems that haven't been identified by the company or to discover whether problems the acquiring company already knows about are greater than it's been told. If the potential acquirer finds either of these scenarios, it uses this as bargaining leverage to change the terms of the deal. In my experience, the potential acquirer tries to do this in about 50 percent of all deals.

Although a term sheet will not be a binding agreement, there's often an accompanying letter that contains a binding no-shop clause. In it, the company agrees not to continue acquisition discussions with any other entity for a period of time, such as 30 days. When a target company enters into a no-shop agreement, it's difficult to find another acquirer if the proposed deal doesn't happen. Experienced acquirers know this and use it as leverage whenever they can.

Handling Negotiations

During the no-shop period and while the due diligence study is continuing, the target company and the potential acquirer negotiate definitive agreements that include terms relating to the structure of the deal, such as a merger or a purchase of assets and assumption of liabilities; the purchase price for the stock or the assets; and the mode of payment, such as stock, cash, notes or a combination of all three. In addition, employment agreements are negotiated for key members of the company's management team, and a disposition is made of the company's outstanding stock options. Often, several agreements have to be renegotiated with the company's suppliers and lenders.

Then the company has to get its own shareholders to approve the deal. This is complicated when there are different classes of stock, as there almost always are in a company financed with venture capital. The time frame for an acquisition like this, from the date of receipt of a term sheet to the closing, is at least 45 days and often 90 days. I've had many CEOs tell me the potential acquirer advised them it could close the deal in 20 days. I've never seen a deal involving a company financed with venture capital close in that short a time.

Last-minute Problems

There are almost always problems that have to be resolved before a deal like this closes. Some of the problems are "deal killers" and others merely affect the valuation. For instance, ownership of the company's intellectual property is not as clear as the company's management believes it to be. Key technical people need to have an incentive to stay after the transaction. Or disgruntled shareholders threaten to take action to prevent the deal from happening. As I often tell young associates in my law firm, there's no such thing as an "easy deal," no matter how smooth things seem at the outset.

Invariably, there will be problems with the definitive agreements. Sometimes the CEO is upset with some of the terms in the definitive agreements, usually because he or she doesn't understand why the acquirer has included these provisions. The CEO tries to negotiate changes to these terms, using up precious negotiating "capital" over insignificant matters when it should be saved for the most significant issues. In other words, CEOs should pick their battles. The term sheet never covers all the issues that are bound to arise when the definitive agreements are negotiated.

Too often, CEOs and boards of development-stage companies have never directly participated in an acquisition before and suffer from "you don't know what you don't know." Because of their inexperience, they sometimes make demands that simply turn off the potential acquirer. As a result, an acquisition that could have allowed creditors to be paid and investors to recover their money fails to take place.

Advice to CEOs

No CEO is perfect. Further, no board of directors is perfect, and it follows there's no such thing as a perfect company. So I offer these tips for anyone who is already a CEO of a development-stage company or aspires to become one.

- **Develop a well-thought-out business strategy for the company.** State it simply and clearly. Most books I've read on the subject are hopelessly vague when it comes to developing and stating a strategy for a development-stage company. Make sure every person reporting to you knows the statement of strategy. A statement such as, "We will be the lowest-cost, highest-quality producer of cable modems, selling the modems only through cable television companies" is grossly inadequate and reflects little thinking about competition, technology, intellectual property, marketing and capital required. A better statement might be: "We will develop and license software for use by medical professionals that helps them keep records of their diagnoses and communicate their instructions to patients. We will develop brand awareness through participation in trade shows and mentions in publications aimed at medical professionals. We will avoid complexity in our software and price it well below competitive products with annual upgrades, for a fee, that have significant value to the user. We will install our software only in the Southeastern United States until we have confidence in our ability to support the software, and then we will expand one region at a time."
- **Review the strategy statement with the board of directors and get a resolution adopting it.** Point out to the board that the strategy statement will have to be adjusted as conditions change in the marketplace.

- **Reserve at least 50 percent of the time during regular board meetings for discussing strategic issues.** Itemize these issues in a memorandum sent to each board member at least one week before the meeting, and provide a brief discussion of each.
- **Send an information package to each board member at least one week before each regular board meeting.** Agree with the board about the information that will be contained in the package. Never provide the board package at the beginning of the meeting because that won't allow directors to be sufficiently prepared.
- **If you're the founder or one of the founders of the company, accept that you work for the board of directors and the board does not work for you.** If you think the board is more of a burden than a benefit, you need an attitude change – and probably a change in the make-up of the board.
- **Get the board's input on strategic issues.** Discussions of strategy with the board should cover the risks the company faces and actions being taken to minimize them.
- **Encourage board members to take their role seriously.** Ask them to attend a seminar about serving as a director, sponsored by the National Association of Corporate Directors or a comparable organization. Subscribe to a publication such as "Board Member" for each member of the board.
- **Stay focused.** If you have trouble doing this, enlist the aid of one of your experienced board members. Entrepreneurs have a difficult time staying focused. Even experienced executives who become entrepreneurs suddenly lose this ability. If you're not focused, you can be sure other key executives in your organization aren't either.
- **Make sure all the people reporting to you are as focused as you are on the functions they are to perform.** Even the most talented executives have a tendency to spend 80 percent of their time on those matters that contribute less than 20 percent to the value of their role.
- **Join an organization made up of other CEOs or senior executives outside your company.** Most CEOs have no one they can talk to inside their companies, especially in the development stage. CEOs have to make difficult decisions and often can't discuss these with other employees of the company. There are various groups for CEOs in each major city.
- **Don't let the board of directors micromanage the company.** This can be a difficult task, especially when there's more than one director who

insists on micromanaging. Take micromanaging directors aside individually and ask them to focus on strategic matters. Ask the directors who are not trying to micromanage to control the agenda at board meetings to cut down on micromanaging.

- **Be squeaky-clean about ethical matters.** Even the smallest breach of ethics, such as charging personal items to the company when traveling, becomes known quickly throughout the company and sets the stage for unethical behavior by lower-ranking employees.
- **Insist the company comply with agreements it has made.** If the CEO has an attitude that any agreement can be breached, this attitude will permeate the organization. A company with this attitude is likely to be careless about entering agreements. Carelessly drawn agreements almost always lead to costly mistakes.
- **Don't obsess over preparing the annual budget.** Everyone knows that a week after the budget has been adopted, conditions will change. Build flexibility into your budget with explanations for changing various items. But there shouldn't be an obsessive requirement to report actual expenses compared to the original budget when, in fact, circumstances have changed.
- **Don't employ your relatives.** Nepotism almost always starts at the CEO level. It can have insidious effects on a company and its employees and is never, ever the right thing to do if there are shareholders other than the CEO and his or her family members.
- **Avoid conflicts of interest.** For instance, requiring your employees to do business with someone who's your relative or friend has negative effects on the company.
- **At the first sign of financial difficulty, consult outside advisors.** Recognize that you, as CEO, might be in denial about impending financial problems. Face the problems as early as possible, before they become crises.
- **Use great care in hiring other executives such as a vice president of marketing or a vice president of engineering or a chief financial officer.** Hire an executive recruiting firm. If you can't afford the fees of a national firm, use a local one that has the skills to interview people and find qualified candidates. Recognize that you simply don't have the interviewing skills needed or the time to check out candidates thoroughly. Your time is worth at least $200 per hour. Therefore, if you can hire someone at $75 per hour to screen candidates and check out their

backgrounds, you're conserving company resources.

- **As painful as this can be, meet monthly with each employee who reports to you to evaluate his or her performance.** Don't fall into the trap of always praising the employee at these evaluation meetings. Every employee has at least one area that could be improved. Make sure you point out this area in a constructive way and offer a solution, such as a management seminar to help the employee improve skills. Make sure you comment about whether the employee is staying focused.
- **When the performance of a key employee disappoints you, make sure you analyze your expectations before you conclude it's solely the employee's fault.** It's very likely you never clearly stated your expectations. Take time now to tell the employee what you expect and give him or her an opportunity to perform. If the employee doesn't meet those expectations within a short period of time, then the person needs to be terminated.
- **Don't be afraid to ask for help in handling personnel issues.** I believe CEOs develop more ulcers from worrying about a non-performing key employee than over any other matter. If you find it difficult to terminate an employee who reports to you, get help from a member of your board of directors, your lawyer or a trusted advisor.
- **Keep the firing process simple.** When terminating a key employee, prepare a severance package in writing, meet the employee in his or her office, and keep the conversation very short. Simply say the employee has not been performing satisfactorily and that you've found it necessary to replace him or her. Hand the person the termination package and ask the employee to coordinate his or her departure with another designated employee. State that an announcement will be made to other employees the next morning that will simply state: "Ms. Smith is leaving the company and we wish her well." The simpler you make this, the better off you and the employee will be.
- **Don't spend too much time on personnel issues.** When you first have the urge to terminate a key employee who reports to you, don't struggle with that urge for more than 30 days. If you still have the urge at the end of 30 days, terminate the employee no matter how painful it is to you.
- **Expect to be compensated fairly for the size of your company.** Performance-based bonuses are always acceptable. The performance factors should relate to achievement of milestones in the business plan.

- **Propose that stock options for you be based on performance.** Make the proposal to the board of directors or to the compensation committee, if there is one, at an appropriate time in writing well before the meeting where the compensation will be discussed. Talk to each director individually before the meeting to gain a sense of what reactions you might see. Try to develop a champion among the directors. Without a champion, your proposal might be poorly received.
- **Trust your key employees, advisors and members of your board of directors.** If you distrust any of them, terminate the relationship if you can. (You can't terminate the director; only shareholders can remove a director.) As CEO, you must be able to trust your advisors to overcome the "you don't know what you don't know" syndrome.
- **Simplify every process in the company and make the executives who report to you simplify every process under their control.** If all processes are kept simple, employees can stay focused on the highest-value activities within their individual functions. As an example, don't go through a major exercise to customize a 401(k) plan where the customization primarily benefits the highly paid executives. Take a simple, standard 401(k) plan from a financial institution and offer it to your employees. Do the same with health insurance. Go to the health insurance provider in your area that has the greatest market share and rely on competition to keep the premiums competitive. Shopping around for the cheapest health insurance provider is a perfect example of saving pennies and squandering dollars when it comes to executive time and employee annoyance.
- **Encourage each executive who reports to you to push the envelope with creative ideas but prepare for rejection.** To keep everyone focused, including yourself, one of your primary missions is to say "no" to many proposals because they don't fit with the company's strategy.
- **Go to experienced professionals for help in raising capital.** Depending on the size of the company, you might turn to an investment banker if you're large enough. Otherwise, make sure you have a very experienced lawyer and an experienced chief financial officer. If you're not large enough to have an experienced CFO, engage a part-time CFO with experience at raising capital.
- **Talk to other entrepreneurs who have raised capital in an amount equal to or more than the amount you intend to raise.** Ask them to describe the pitfalls to you. Raising capital as a privately held company

is the hardest job of a CEO. Trying to raise too much capital will likely result in failing to raise any capital. Raising too little capital will usually cause unhappy investors when the company has to raise more capital on terms that significantly dilute the early investments.

- **Prepare your business plan and keep it current by revising it at least monthly.** The business plan should be prepared so you can actually operate the business under it, not solely for raising capital. Review the business plan with your board at least once every three months.
- **Avoid long-term commitments with suppliers, landlords and others.** Whenever possible, have an escape valve in any agreement that is to last for more than one year, allowing you to terminate the agreement either by paying money or by providing notice. Don't fall for the trap that you can get a lower per-unit price by making a large commitment to buy components for your products. Don't sign office or manufacturing space leases that don't allow you to terminate within a maximum period of one year by either providing for a termination payment or providing for termination notice of six months or longer. Keep every dollar of capital you can available for marketing and sales development.
- **Keep the company's administrative function mean and lean.** When an executive comes to you requesting expenditures for a non-budgeted item or service, ask whether the expenditure is revenue producing or cost reducing. If it is neither, be extraordinarily thorough in analyzing whether the expenditure is absolutely necessary.
- **When making financial projections, focus on the revenue line and all the factors that must be considered to predict future revenues.** Most companies have no way of knowing what their revenues will be three months out, let alone five years out. The best they can do is to make expenditures intended to develop revenues and hope the revenues develop at the rate predicted. Revenue projections should be based on the expenditures that will cause the revenues to be generated, such as sales contacts, development of value-added resellers, plans to sell to original equipment manufacturers and so forth. CEOs and CFOs who show me business plans with revenues increasing at the rate of, say, 20 percent per year get an F for business planning unless they can show me the expenditures being made today that will cause revenues to be generated tomorrow.
- **Don't understaff the accounting function.** Keep in mind the primary function for the accounting department is to pay bills, manage payroll

and collect receivables. If those functions are not adequately staffed, how can you possibly expect the controller or the chief financial officer to be effective in any planning process? If you want real help from your controller or chief financial officer in business planning, make sure that person can spend at least 30 percent of his or her time performing this function. My observation is that most CEOs have disdain for the accounting function and keep that function grossly understaffed. Then the CEOs complain they don't get appropriate planning help from the controller or the chief financial officer.

- **Spend at least 50 percent of your time in front of customers or potential customers.** There is no substitute for the CEO being engaged firsthand with people and organizations that can purchase the product.
- **Make sure you have qualified outside directors on your board.** It's difficult to appoint strangers to your board and have the trust that's necessary. However, if you consider only your acquaintances, you won't have a sufficient number of qualified candidates. Rely on your advisors and other directors to suggest candidates who will be courageous enough to speak their mind. Develop a board that will challenge your strategy yet be supportive of you once decisions are made.
- **Be skeptical about the value of stock options for workers other than key employees.** Stock options can be incredibly dilutive to shareholders. They do act as "glue" for some employees who are considering whether to leave the company if there are unvested options. But below a certain level of management, my experience is that stock options are not a motivator to perform. It's time to rethink the standard formula that 20 percent of the outstanding shares in the company should be set aside for stock options for key employees, including the CEO if that person is not one of the founders. In my opinion, probably half of the stock options under this formula are wasted because they don't motivate the option holders to improve the company's performance.
- **If you're not the founder of the company, be prepared for the founder to try to have you fired no matter how supportive he or she seems to be.** If you don't have the solid backing of a majority of the members of the board, not including the founder, you're likely to be in trouble.
- **If you've never developed a written business strategy before, ask for advice from one or more CEOs who have.** It's highly unlikely you can find a consultant who will do this for you unless you're willing to pay a huge

price, which is usually prohibitive for development-stage companies.

- **Make each executive who reports to you give you a bullet-point list of his or her major duties weighted as to value to the company.** Reach agreement with each executive about the bullet points and the weights assigned. Tell these executives they should spend their time according to the weighting on the bullet points. This will help each executive keep things simple and focus on those activities that have the greatest weight.
- **Learn to delegate authority carefully.** Make sure any agreement involving an expenditure above a certain amount is personally reviewed by you or by the company's lawyer. You or the attorney should also review contracts for any commitment of longer than 12 months, including any employment agreement.
- **Compensate your employees at 10 percent above the going rate across the board.** Make it difficult for any employee to leave over compensation. The 10 percent premium is small compared with the expense the company must go through to replace an employee who leaves because he or she was offered higher compensation.
- **Keep in mind that companies cannot grow without capital.** The rule of thumb for technology companies is that it takes $100,000 of capital for every new employee. Most companies fail if they try to grow at a high rate while undercapitalized. On the other hand, most companies can't raise capital until they have achieved some level of customer traction. I know that's a Catch-22.
- **Understand the major market forces that affect your operation.** Companies don't succeed because they have an employee handbook or a widespread stock option program or incredibly detailed budgets and the like. They succeed because they've taken advantage of major market forces for their product or service. Your function as CEO is to know exactly what these forces are and how you can make these forces work for the company. If you fail to understand these forces, you will fail as a CEO.
- **Know how to use consultants and outside professionals, such as lawyers.** Make sure you and your professionals understand the S curve. Tell them in no uncertain terms where you expect them to work on the S curve.
- **Clearly understand the difference between customer demand and customer need as perceived by your engineering team.** The engineer-

ing team almost always equates its perception of customer need with customer demand. Yet, there is usually a giant disconnect between this perception and actual demand. Your job is to make sure your chief marketing or sales officer knows the difference and can tell you what outside forces can come to bear to create demand for your product or service. Development-stage companies simply don't have the resources to create demand for their products or services. Demand is created by outside forces.

- **If you're developing a new technology or a significantly improved technology that will require adoption by the customer base, recognize that predicting the rate of adoption is almost impossible.** Keep the company lean and mean until there's actual adoption by a number of customers. Spending marketing and sales dollars thinking the adoption rate can be accelerated is a waste of money.
- **Don't be fooled by the testimony of early adopters of your technology if your company is in a high-tech field.** The rate of adoption by early adopters often misleads companies into ramping up overhead and marketing for a product or service before the real market has developed.
- **Don't have a fancy office.** It's almost inevitable when a person is appointed CEO, he or she insists on buying new office furniture, followed by new reception area furniture. It's like a disease CEOs catch. This sends a message to employees that the CEO isn't cost conscious in his or her own area while trying to make all others curb costs. This is a bad message. A CEO in a development-stage company who must have nice office furnishings needs to re-examine his or her priorities.

Advice to Outside Board Members

Often, men and women who are appointed to the boards of development-stage companies or small-cap publicly held companies have never served on a board before. Most directors are acquaintances of the CEO or selected by the CEO because they're acquainted with another director or an advisor to the company. They're keenly aware they're serving on the board at the pleasure of the CEO – although technically, only shareholders can remove a director. If you're in this position, here's my advice.

- **If you don't already know the company's business well, get to know it.** Read trade publications or any other written materials that will give you a good background.
- **Make sure the company indemnifies you by a provision in the Articles of Incorporation, the bylaws or a separate agreement.** Indemnification should include mandatory advancement of expenses, which is optional under many state laws.
- **Try to get an idea, in writing, of what the CEO and the other members of the board expect of you as a director.** Make sure you have a clear understanding with the CEO that you have a duty to represent all stockholders and that you *will* ask difficult questions. Try to establish before becoming a director that you'll be diligent in performing your duties.
- **Prepare well by insisting on receiving a board package at least a week before each meeting.** If there's an emergency special meeting, insist the topic be outlined to you in writing with as much notice as possible
- **Make sure you're heard on any issue, especially if you have an opinion that differs with those expressed by other directors.** The reason state law requires a board of directors is to make sure different opinions

are expressed so decisions are considered carefully.

- **Talk to the CEO ahead of time about any matters that trouble you.** Don't surprise the CEO at a board meeting if you're going to object to something the CEO will propose. Likewise, you should not expect surprises from the CEO at board meetings.
- **Insist that at least half of the time for each regular board meeting be spent on discussion of strategic matters.** Don't take part in efforts by other directors to micromanage the company. Point out to other directors when they're trying to micromanage, and state your objection.
- **Make sure the CEO knows what types of items should come before the board for approval and what types are solely within the CEO's authority.** For instance, any item that is contained in a board-approved budget need not come before the board again for approval. On the other hand, an agreement that will commit the company to an expenditure equal to more than 10 percent of its capital should require board approval.
- **If the board develops a laundry list of items or magnitudes of matters that must come before the directors, make sure that list is not too detailed.** Give the CEO the right to exercise some judgment about what comes before the board. It's better to have a set of principles about matters requiring board approval than to have a detailed set of rules.
- **Attend all meetings.** If you can't attend in person, be present by conference telephone. All states allow directors to attend meetings by conference telephone where they can hear the others speak and the others can hear them speak. It's wise to have a provision in the bylaws that any director has the right to participate by telephone conference with the company paying for the call. It's not enough that the bylaws simply authorize meetings by conference telephone.
- **Have the courage to express dissent.** You'll be surprised how expressing dissent the first time will cause the CEO and other board members to think very hard about getting your support on a matter before a board meeting. Further, if you discuss your reasons for opposing certain matters before the board meeting, you'll be surprised how the CEO and other directors are willing to adapt whatever action is proposed to gain your support. Nevertheless, you need to draw a line and dissent when necessary.
- **You don't necessarily have to vote against a motion to express your dissent.** You can abstain. If you want to vote yes but have reservations,

ask that the minutes reflect your reservations.

- **You really do have to look out for shareholders and not just the person who caused your appointment, the CEO.** If the CEO is a founder of the company and owns a large number of shares, you can't automatically assume that whatever the CEO favors is in the best interest of all stockholders. If you have an argument against a certain action and express it in terms of not being in the best interest of stockholders, you'll get much more attention for your argument.
- **Make sure you understand the major accounting issues that face the company.** If there are deferred expenses or accelerated revenues, make sure you know the auditing firm agrees with the company's expense deferral and revenue recognition policies. Don't simply rely on the audit committee's view of these major matters.
- **Don't be afraid to ask hard questions.** By asking the so-called tough questions at board meetings, you'll act as an invisible hand over the entire company, preventing the company from doing stupid things. Whenever members of management make presentations to the board, make sure you ask penetrating questions. You'll be surprised at how seriously members of management take questions asked of them by directors. On the other hand, asking questions about insignificant or irrelevant matters will detract from your value as an invisible hand.
- **Listen to the opinions of other directors.** Reasonable people can differ. Reserve the right to change your mind at a board meeting. Even though you might have already expressed your opinion to the CEO or other directors before the board meeting, other directors might still persuade you to support another view.
- **Make sure enough time is set aside for each board meeting.** Try to get other directors to make their travel plans so as not to place artificial limits on how long board meetings can go. Try to get the heaviest issues at the head of the agenda rather than letting them come under "other business" at the end of the meeting.
- **Don't seek to be compensated as a consultant.** As soon as you're compensated for services other than serving as a director, you have compromised your independence.
- **Keep your ego in check.** Don't allow yourself to feel attacked when another director disagrees with you.
- **Don't be pressured into making a major decision in a short time frame.** CEOs often allow certain matters to reach the crisis level before

bringing the matters to the board for resolution. Have the courage to seek more time and information.

- **Make sure the CEO's compensation is reasonable for the size of the company.** There are good sources of information on compensation. For electronics companies, the American Electronics Association has an annual survey of compensation that's an excellent source for compensation of CEOs and others for various sizes of companies. If the CEO is a founder, *do not* grant options to the founder. If the founder's interests are not already aligned with those of the other shareholders because of the founder's ownership of stock, options will not further align the founder's interests.
- **Make sure you understand the major risks facing the company.** All companies are fragile. What could cause the company to be in severe difficulties in a short period of time? What is being done to mitigate these risks?
- **You're entitled to reasonable compensation as a director.** What is reasonable? Unfortunately, the risk usually far outweighs the reward for serving as a director of a development-stage company. I suggest that outside directors receive cash compensation as well as stock options. The way I try to determine compensation is to establish a fair hourly rate for the board member, then assume there will be at least 12 hours devoted to each board meeting – eight hours at the meeting and four hours to prepare. I also assume there will be at least two or three special board meetings during the year at two hours per board meeting. If the company is having only quarterly regular meetings, this means there will be four meetings at 12 hours each and two special meetings at two hours each, by telephone, for 52 hours. If the appropriate hourly rate for the person is $200 per hour, then the director ought to receive at least $10,400 per year – probably rounded up to $11,000. I also recommend a stock option equal to one-half of 1 percent of the outstanding shares in the company, vesting over three years at the rate of 1/36 per month as long as the person is serving as a member of the board of directors. You should receive additional compensation for serving on a committee, using the same method for determining the compensation. Of course, board compensation varies significantly from company to company.
- **Attend the dinner that usually precedes or follows the board meeting to socialize with the other directors and members of management.** This is a good way to gain added information from management

that's not otherwise available to you, and to better understand where each director is coming from.

- **Make a modest investment in the company.** If you don't think the company is worthy of you making a modest investment, say $20,000, you shouldn't serve on its board.
- **If you're going to be a member of the audit committee of a publicly held company, make sure you know what you're getting into.** Audit committee members must now struggle with how to limit the time they spend on this function. Their responsibilities are essentially open-ended because of the Sarbanes-Oxley Act.
- **Written consents by the board require unanimous consent because there is no discussion about the matter.** If you think discussion is required before you sign a written consent, make sure the other directors know you want to have a meeting by telephone or face to face to discuss your concerns. Don't sign the written consent if you have any concerns about the matter.
- **Have confidence in your own knowledge.** Even though you might not be an expert on the technology developed by the company, and you might not be a marketing or financial expert, if the CEO or CFO can't express things in simple, businesslike terms and make compelling arguments for an action to be taken, don't vote in favor of the action.
- **Insist on fairly detailed minutes.** There's always a difference of opinion about how minutes should be kept. Lawyers who litigate argue the minutes should be kept to a bare minimum because they'll have to be produced in any litigation. Corporate lawyers who want to make sure the business reasons for taking various actions are clearly stated want the minutes to be in great detail. There's a compromise somewhere between these two positions. Management often looks back at the minutes to determine what the board decided. If the minutes are bare-bones, they don't provide guidance to management. I recommend the basic reasons for an action taken by the board be summarized in the minutes along with the actual resolution.
- **Talk to shareholders.** Try to understand their expectations. You represent the shareholders. You should know how they feel about matters. On the other hand, only you, as a board member, will have sufficient information to make most major decisions affecting the shareholders, who typically don't have all the information necessary to make decisions.
- **Use your common sense when dealing with board matters.** Common

sense applies even to the most complicated issues.

- **Invest in your education as a board member.** Attend a seminar for directors within 12 months of becoming a director, and every other year thereafter. Become a member of the National Association of Directors or a comparable organization. Read the pamphlet published by the American Bar Association about being a director.
- **If the company is publicly held, meet with the other outside directors outside the presence of the inside directors after every regular board meeting to discuss concerns that might not have been expressed at the board meeting.** Appoint a lead director to act as the communicator with the CEO and other directors. Meetings like this will be threatening to the CEO, the CFO and, perhaps, the general counsel to the company.
- **Help the board reach a balance between asking tough questions and being supportive of the management team.** All boards need to have a healthy tension between the board and the management team. When the board becomes too adversarial or too supportive, it becomes ineffective.
- **Never waive a conflict of interest for an executive officer or board member without an incredibly compelling reason.** Even then, do this only after requiring that the conflict be monitored by an independent law firm or accounting firm with periodic reports to the board.
- **Share this information.** If you're going to be an outside director on the board of a development-stage company or a small-cap publicly held company, you might want to give this list to the CEO or other directors to get their comments on the various bullet points. You'll smoke out their views on these matters quickly.

Glossary

The following business terms are used in this book. In addition to their definitions, I've also included an example of each term used in one or two sentences.

ACCELERATED REVENUES – Revenues that have been created through extraordinary measures to ship products or induce customers to take early delivery of products. Another form of accelerated revenues is when a company accounts for software license fees up front even though delivery to the customer does not signal the end of work the company is responsible for handling. Under most circumstances, revenues should be recognized only after the work has been completed. *The company accelerated revenues by offering distributors discounts for taking delivery of products before the end of the quarter. This occurred when there was no other business reason for offering the discounts.*

ACCOUNTS PAYABLE – Invoices for products or services that have been received but for which payment has not been made. *The company typically paid its accounts payable in 45 days rather than 30 days as requested by its vendors.*

ACCOUNTS RECEIVABLE – Amounts to be paid by customers for goods or services already delivered for which payment has not been received. *The company typically collected its accounts receivable on average within 60 days after invoicing the customer.*

ACQUISITION – Acquiring a company by purchasing the assets and assuming liabilities, or merging the target company into a subsidiary of the acquiring company, or purchasing all of the stock in the target company, or some other acquisition form. *The company is seeking an acquisition in an area that would be complementary to its product line.*

ADOPTION PERIOD – When a company introduces a new technology to the marketplace, the period of time before the marketplace starts using the technology in the ordinary course of business. *The company predicted the adoption period for its new voice recognition technology would be two years.*

AMORTIZE – To spread the cost of something over a period of time, from an accounting viewpoint. *The company allocated $500,000 to goodwill it purchased in connection with the acquisition of the widget company and elected to amortize this goodwill over a 10-year period at the rate of 10 percent per year.*

ANGEL INVESTOR – An investor not related to company founders who is willing to purchase stock, or a note that is convertible into stock, or a note that has warrants so it may become equity in the future. Most angel investors are wealthy individuals with a net worth of at least $1 million, although investors with a net worth less than this are known to make significant investments in young companies. *The company is seeking angel investors to raise $500,000 initially with a $100,000 minimum investment by each.*

AUDIT COMMITTEE – A committee of the board of directors of a company that is large enough to need annual audits and a separate committee to work with the auditors. All publicly held companies are required to have audit committees, and most companies with venture capital firms as investors are contractually required to have annual audited financial statements and an audit committee. *The company's board of directors appointed three of the outside directors as members of the audit committee responsible for overseeing the audit and periodically meeting with the auditing firm.*

BACKLOG – Orders received by the company that have not yet been filled. Some businesses have large backlogs and others have none. When a company has a backlog, it can usually manage its expenses better than a company that has no backlog. *The company increased its backlog from $200,000 to $300,000 as of the end of the most recent quarter versus the previous quarter.*

BREAK–EVEN POINT – The point at which the rate of revenues equals the rate of expenses for a company. Start-up companies operate at a loss initially and prepare a forecast of when revenues will be at a rate that covers its expenses. *The company believed it would be at the break-even point within six months.*

BURN RATE – The monthly rate of expenses for the company. This rate is usually measured in terms of cash rather than expenses, from an accounting viewpoint, since expenses might include non-cash elements. *The company increased its burn rate from $300,000 per month to $400,000 in anticipation of a ramp-up in sales.*

CAPITAL INVESTMENT – Purchase of an asset that will be used for a significant period of time. Companies make capital investments in items such as computers, software, test equipment, leasehold improvements and furniture. *The company intends to make capital investments of more than $300,000 over the next quarter by purchasing additional servers for its network.*

CAPITALIZE – To accumulate expenses and treat the total as an asset to be amortized over accounting periods in the future. Under certain circumstances, the accounting rules permit a company to capitalize expenses so the accounting charges are incurred in the future rather than at the time the expenses are actually made. *The company spent $200,000 on using its computer programmers to develop an accounting software package for keeping track of travel expenses and decided to capitalize this expenditure and amortize it over a three-year period, the estimated life of the computer software.*

CHAPTER 11 PETITION – A filing with a federal bankruptcy court that initiates Chapter 11 reorganization proceedings. *The company decided to file a Chapter 11 Petition after its bank froze its checking account when the company defaulted on its loan payment.*

CONVERTIBLE NOTES – A note is a promise to pay money, often referred to as a promissory note. A convertible note is one that can be converted, at the election of the lender, into equity in the company. The terms under which the note may be converted are usually set forth in the convertible note. *The company offered convertible notes to angel investors in order to raise $1.5 million of capital.*

CORPORATE OPPORTUNITY DOCTRINE – Under the law for the state in which the company is incorporated, the duty of officers and directors to give the company the first right to take advantage of any business opportunities related to the company's business. An officer or director who takes advantage of a business opportunity related to the company's business without disclosing it to the company and giving the company the first right is breaching the corporate opportunity doctrine and may be liable for damages or other remedies for the company. *Mr. Smith, who served on the board* *of directors of Company X, invested in a new company making a competing and possibly better product than Company X. He did not disclose his investment to Company X, and when other directors learned of this, Company X filed a lawsuit against him for violating the corporate opportunity doctrine.*

DEFERRED EXPENSES – To put off or delay certain expenses, often by using questionable accounting practices, in order to enhance the profits of a particular quarter or fiscal year. *The company paid for certain advertising that had already taken place, but decided to defer this expense to the following quarter on the theory that the advertising would benefit the following quarter.*

DEVELOPMENT-STAGE COMPANY – A company that has not yet received significant revenues or that is incurring losses as part of the start-up plan of the company. Some companies can be in the development stage for a number of years, and even young publicly held companies can still be in the development stage. *The company was in the development stage and seeking investors for at least $2 million, which the founders projected would take it to a profitable operation.*

DISTRIBUTION CHANNEL – A method used by the company to sell its products or services. Some companies sell their products or services directly to the purchasers using an internal sales force. Others use distributors to purchase the company's products and resell them. Still others use resellers who incorporate the company's products into other systems sold by the reseller. Each of these methods is referred to as a distribution channel. *The company decided to use a new distribution channel by selling its products to major distributors in Europe.*

DUE DILIGENCE – A thorough review of a company's background, including its books, records, contracts, customers and business practices, usually in connection with an impending acquisition of the company. *After reaching a preliminary understanding of the terms of acquiring the company, the purchaser decided to perform extensive due diligence on the company before closing on the transaction.*

EARLY ADOPTERS – Usually in connection with a technology, those persons who are interested in using the very latest even though it might be unproven. *The company expected early adopters to purchase its new product but would not base its sales forecast on their purchases. Instead, the company would use great care in forecasting sales only after the product was being purchased by ordinary consumers.*

EQUITY CAPITAL – Money invested in a company by purchasers of stock. This money is invested in the form of common stock, preferred stock or convertible preferred stock. Unlike money a company borrows and must repay, equity capital does not have to be repaid to the investors. *The company is seeking $2 million in equity capital from venture capital firms and is prepared to sell convertible preferred stock rather than common stock if the venture capital firms require this.*

EXECUTIVE PLACEMENT FIRM – Commonly referred to as "headhunters," firms that help companies fill executive positions by approaching executives who often are not looking to leave their current employer. Executive placement firms usually work for a fixed fee and sometimes a combination of a fixed fee plus a contingent fee based on success. *The company engaged an executive placement firm to find the best possible candidate for vice president of marketing.*

FIDUCIARY DUTY – A duty to use care in business matters at the same level a prudent person would use in the same position and under the same circumstances. Officers and directors owe a fiduciary duty to the company and its stockholders. *The board of directors of the company was accused of breaching its fiduciary duty to the stockholders when it approved a very large severance package for an executive officer who had been with the company for only three months.*

FINANCIAL PROJECTIONS – Projections of revenues, expenses and balance sheets for periods in the future such as monthly, quarterly or yearly, often for three to five years, based on assumptions the company believes are reasonable. *The company prepared financial projections for the next three years, based on assumed revenues and projected expenses, and projected the balance sheets for the end of each quarter during that period as a way to show investors the potential profits.*

FINDER – A person who has contacts with prospective investors and introduces the company to them, receiving a finder's fee if they invest, generally in the vicinity of 3 percent of the amount of the investment. There are legitimate finders, but many persons who claim to be finders are con artists who prey on young companies by requiring a substantial fee such as $25,000 to be paid up front for introductions to Mid-East or South American investors. The introductions never bear fruit. *The company was approached by a finder who promised he could raise $2 million for the company* *from investors in Saudi Arabia, but would charge a fee of 10 percent of the amount of the investment plus an ongoing consultant fee of $10,000 a month for 24 months.*

FLOATING CONVERTIBLE PRICE – The price per share used to determine the number of shares into which a convertible note may be converted where the price per share "floats" with the average closing price per share for a certain period of time, such as five business days. This can be used only for companies that are publicly held. *The company issued convertible notes with a floating convertible price determined by multiplying 0.85 times the average closing price of the trailing five business days before the notice of conversion is received by the company.*

FOLLOWER STRATEGY – A development-stage company's strategy to follow in the footsteps of a large company that is developing a new market. The large company makes the expenditures necessary to educate the market. The development-stage company tries to find a narrow segment of the market and develop a product for it that is not offered by the larger company. *The company knew IBM was developing software to allow hospitals to create patient records electronically and decided to focus its activities on a product that would use the IBM software but focus on specific groups within hospitals, such as emergency room physicians.*

GENERALLY ACCEPTED ACCOUNTING PRINCIPLES (GAAP) – The accounting principles adopted by the Financial Accounting Standards Board for the United States and used by all companies and accounting firms to account for various transactions, assets, liabilities and expenses. An auditor can't sign off on an audit for a company unless the company's financial statements comply with GAAP. *The company failed to comply with GAAP in its financial projections to investors, and some of the investors developed a sense of distrust for the company's financial statements as a result.*

GUIDANCE – In publicly held companies, providing securities analysts and the public with estimates of next-quarter or fiscal year earnings per share. *The company's CFO provided guidance for the current fiscal year of 30 cents per share, knowing that the company's internal projections indicated the company might earn 33 cents per share. The CFO wanted to provide guidance that was lower than what he thought the company would actually achieve.*

"HOCKEY STICK" REVENUE CURVE – In graphical form, a revenue line that looks like a hockey stick on its side with the part used to strike the puck to the right and pointing upward. All young companies project a slow growth in revenues initially, while they're in the development stage, followed by a rapid increase in revenues at some point in order to impress investors with the company's predicted performance. *The company's projections showed the usual hockey stick revenue curve, with revenues developing slowly within the first 18 months and then taking off.*

HOSTILE TAKEOVER – An unsolicited offer to acquire the company where the board of directors of the company opposes the acquisition. *The company was acquired in a hostile takeover even though the company's board of directors opposed the deal. A majority of the shareholders voted in favor of the acquisition.*

INDEPENDENT DIRECTOR – A member of the board of directors who does not hold an officer position in the company and has no affiliation with the company that involves being paid or having influence over spending. The term is defined under the rules of the New York Stock Exchange, the American Stock Exchange and Nasdaq, as well as in the Securities Exchange Act of 1934. *The company has a board of directors of five persons, including three independent directors.*

INITIAL PUBLIC OFFERING (IPO) – The company's first sale of stock to the public, which takes place after the company files a registration statement with the U.S. Securities and Exchange Commission. In the initial public offering, only those shares that are actually sold in the public offering are registered, meaning other shares that remain outstanding in the company – usually more than a majority – are not registered for sale. *The company met with several investment banking firms to select one of them to underwrite its initial public offering, which involved selling $30 million worth of stock to the public.*

INSIDE DIRECTOR – A member of the board of directors who is an officer, key employee, or advisor of the company. This person differs from an independent director because he or she receives compensation from the company for services other than those of serving as a director, usually as a senior officer of the company. *The company's board of directors consists of five people, including two inside directors.*

"INVISIBLE HAND" – A term found in Adam Smith's book *Wealth of Nations*, indicating that capitalism places an "invisible hand" over the economy, allocating capital to those areas where the highest return will be earned. In this book, I use the term "invisible hand" to mean the omnipresence of the board of directors over major decisions being made by company officers who know they'll have to defend these decisions before the board. Even though the board is not directly involved in the decision-making, the prospect that the board will challenge the decision makes executive officers use care and diligence. *The company's CEO felt the "invisible hand" of the board of directors as he began negotiations to acquire another company, knowing that the board would scrutinize the proposal when he presented it.*

IRRATIONAL INVESTORS – People who make an investment based on relationships rather than on a critical analysis of the company. Typical irrational investors are relatives, friends and others who base their investment solely on their personal relationship with the company's founders. *The company's initial capital of $100,000 came from several relatives of the founder and the founder's best friend. These irrational investors did not thoroughly analyze the company's business, but made the investment solely on the basis of their personal relationship with the founder.*

"LIVING DEAD" – Companies that are barely staying alive with flat revenues and very small profits, or are in the slow process of dying as revenues decline and losses increase. Often, when the founder realizes the company can't meet the expectations of its investors, the founder turns the company into a means for making a living without any prospect of providing a return to investors. *After raising slightly more than $1 million from friends, family and two angel investors, the company joined the "living dead" when it became evident its product was not competitive with most similar products on the market and that the company lacked the resources to develop new products.*

MARKET INTELLIGENCE – Knowledge about the marketplace to be addressed by the company, including the competitive offerings, the size of different segments of the market, the decision-making process customers go through to purchase products or services, and the economic and technological forces that are affecting this market. *The company relied on anecdotal evidence of the market for its products rather than market intelligence gathered methodically from as many sources as practical.*

MANAGEMENT DISCUSSION AND ANALYSIS (MD&A) – A qualitative analysis of financial statements prepared by publicly held companies. This section of the financial report gives the company's analysis of changes that have occurred and trends that could directly affect the company's financial performance. The MD&A section is required as part of the quarterly and annual filings publicly held companies make with the SEC. *The company's MD&A revealed that its gross margin had declined significantly due to changes in the sales mix of products because lower-margin products made up a greater percentage of the company's sales than those for the previous quarter.*

MINIMUM CONVERSION PRICE – A formula used to turn convertible preferred stock and convertible notes into common stock or, in some cases, a different class of stock, usually on the basis of a conversion price per share. Sometimes the formula is variable, depending on the public market price for the stock at certain points in time or for a trailing period of time. For example, a convertible note could contain a formula saying it could be converted at 85 percent of the company's average closing price on Nasdaq for the previous 10 trading days. Often when a variable conversion formula is involved, a company will insist there be a minimum conversion price as a means of protecting against inordinate dilution. *The company issued convertible notes that could be turned into shares of common stock at a price per share equal to the average closing price for the period of 10 trading days before the election to convert, with a minimum conversion price of $1 per share.*

NET AFTER-TAX PROFITS – The profits earned by a company using generally accepted accounting principles after all taxes have been paid or accounted for. *The company's net after-tax profits increased by 50 percent for the year just ended.*

NO-SHOP CLAUSE – A provision in an agreement that says the company agrees not to solicit or accept any other offers for its purchase for a certain period of time. A no-shop clause is almost always found in acquisition agreements so the acquiring company knows it has the exclusive right to buy the target company on the terms contained in the agreement for a certain period of time. *The no-shop clause gave the buyer the right to purchase the company for $8 million without competing offers for a 90-day period while the buyer conducted due diligence on the company.*

NO-SHOP PERIOD – The length of time of the no-shop clause. Buyers want no-shop provisions that have a long period of time, such as 90 days, so the buyer has adequate time to conduct due diligence. The selling company wants a short period of time for the no-shop clause, such as 20 days. *The company negotiated a 20-day no-shop clause with the buyer, knowing there were others that had an interest in acquiring the company in the event that the* *definitive agreements could not be negotiated with the buyer.*

OFFERING MEMORANDUM – A document prepared by a company used in raising capital from angel investors or venture capital firms. The offering memorandum contains much of the information found in a prospectus for a public offering. *The company prepared an offering memorandum, which made full disclosure of all material facts about the company in order to raise capital from angel investors.*

OVERSIGHT – The duty of the board of directors to watch over the actions of the management team by reviewing the quarterly financial statements and asking hard questions about the company's performance. *The board of directors appointed a three-member committee to conduct oversight of the company's marketing activities to make sure they were conducted in an ethical manner.*

PERIOD EXPENSES – Those types of expenses that must be recognized during a period such as a quarter or fiscal year no matter what the revenues are during that time. These are often referred to as fixed expenses and consist of items such as rent, insurance, salaries and fringe benefits of administrative personnel. *The company argued with its auditors over certain expenses the auditors believed should be period expenses, which the company believed should be deferred until certain related revenues were earned.*

POSITIVE CASH FLOW – Cash the company receives from revenues that exceeds its expenses and capital expenditures. While a company might show a profit from a GAAP standpoint, it might still be operating in a negative cash flow situation, consuming more cash than it is receiving. When a company achieves positive cash flow, it has reached the point where its internally generated cash can be used to fund its growth. *The company projected it would achieve positive cash flow two years after it was founded.*

PREMIUM – The price per share that exceeds the previous price per share paid for stock in the company in its last financing. As an example, if the company had a financing by selling 1 million shares at $3 per share and a second financing by selling 2 million shares at $4 per share, the premium for the last round of financing was $1 per share. *The company's financial projections indicated it would have three rounds of financing, with each round having a premium over the previous round.*

PROGRESS PAYMENT BASIS – An agreement that says the customer makes payments periodically as a project is performed. *The company proposed* *to perform the $5 million project for the customer over two years, with progress payments to be made every quarter according to an agreed-upon schedule.*

PROJECTED BALANCE SHEET – An integral part of projected financial statements that gives a snapshot of the financial condition of the company on a particular date. When making financial projections, it's important for a company to estimate its balance sheets as of certain dates in the future in order to show its anticipated financial condition at those points in time. *The company projected balance sheets for the ending date of each of the next four quarters and each of the next three fiscal years.*

PROXY FIGHT – A situation that arises during the voting process in publicly held companies. Shareholders can vote in person or by proxy on matters coming before them. In publicly held companies, it's usually impractical for most shareholders to attend the meeting to cast their votes. These shareholders grant proxies to designated persons, usually members of the company's top management, which give them the authority to cast votes for those who are absent as outlined in the proxy. A proxy fight develops in a publicly held company when different contenders seek proxies from shareholders who support their position for or against a matter. *A shareholder with 10 percent of the company's outstanding shares decided to launch a proxy fight to replace the board of directors.*

"PUMP AND DUMP" ARTISTS – A term used often by the SEC when it pursues people who pump up the stock price of small publicly held companies through press releases or through blogs, or by buying stock with the intention of moving the price of the stock up, and then sell a large number of shares after creating great interest, causing the stock to promptly fall in price. "Pump and dump" artists use fraudulent means to make large profits in this manner. *The company's stock was traded on the bulletin board, and several "pump and dump" artists attempted to manipulate the price.*

REGULATION S OR REG S OFFERING – An offering of stock outside of the United States to persons who are not U.S. residents. Regulation S was adopted by the U.S. Securities and Exchange Commission to prevent stock sold in this manner from coming onto the U.S. market without complying with certain holding periods and disclosure requirements. *A small investment banker approached the company and proposed that the company make a Reg S offering to investors in the Channel Islands and certain other tax havens outside of the United States.*

RESTART – When investors, usually venture capital firms, rescue a failing company by putting in more money and essentially wiping out the equity interests of the other shareholders. *The company struggled for several years without generating significant revenues even though the product had great promise. Finally, the venture capital investors advised the company they would not put more money into the company unless there was a restart.*

REVENUE PROJECTIONS – Projections a company makes about its future sales of either products or services. *The company's revenue projections showed it would have total revenues in its third fiscal year of $6 million.*

SARBANES-OXLEY ACT – A federal law enacted in 2002 creating a commission to oversee accounting firms doing audit work for publicly held companies and imposing certain additional duties on CEOs and CFOs of publicly held companies with respect to their financial statements. *Under the Sarbanes-Oxley Act, the CEO must certify that to his knowledge, the financial statements filed with the SEC fairly present the financial condition of the company.*

SEC REGULATION FD – A fair disclosure measure the SEC adopted in 2000 to prevent companies from disclosing material facts to securities analysts and others before making such disclosures to the entire marketplace. Regulation FD now requires companies to immediately publish all disclosures it makes to securities analysts and others of a material nature concerning the company's financial performance, usually by issuing a press release containing the information. *When the company invited several securities analysts to a private meeting, it used great care in immediately issuing a press release about the information it had provided to them so the entire market had the same information.*

SECURITIES ANALYST – A person with an investment banking firm who writes reports about the merits of buying, or not buying, stock in specific publicly held companies. *After the company's IPO, several securities analysts wrote reports about the company recommending that investors purchase the company's stock.*

SECURITIES AND EXCHANGE COMMISSION (SEC) – A federal agency that oversees all securities dealers, stock exchanges and publicly held companies. *The SEC advised the company it had launched an investigation into certain transactions in the company's stock that occurred shortly before the company announced it would be acquired.*

SERIES A – The first round of significant capital raised by the company, usually with venture capital firms, and sometimes with angel investors. The term comes from the preferred stock that is usually issued in connection with this financing, Series A Convertible Preferred Stock. *The company had a Series A round of financing for $2 million, funded by three venture capital firms.*

SERIES A CONVERTIBLE PREFERRED STOCK – Stock in a company that has some type of preference over the common stock or other classes or series of preferred stock, usually a preference in the liquidation of the company. Convertible preferred stock can be converted by the holder into shares of common stock according to a predetermined formula. Series A Convertible Preferred Stock is the name usually given to the first series of convertible preferred stock issued by a company. Subsequent series usually follow in terms of Series B, Series C, Series D. *The venture capital firms purchased Series B Convertible Preferred Stock in the Series B round of financing for a total of $3 million.*

SMALL-CAP – A term used for a publicly held company with a market capitalization of less than a certain amount. Securities analysts and investors categorize publicly held companies as large-cap, medium-cap, small-cap or micro-cap, depending on the total value of the company's outstanding stock. The value is determined by multiplying the number of shares outstanding by the closing price of the stock on a specific market such as Nasdaq or the New York Stock Exchange. Some analysts view companies with a total market capitalization, or market cap, of $500 million or less as a small-cap company. Other securities analysts use $100 million as the cutoff for a small-cap company. *The business is a small-cap company listed on Nasdaq because its total market capitalization is approximately $50 million.*

STOCK OPTION – A contractual right to purchase stock at a fixed price over a certain period of time. A vested stock option may be exercised at any time. An unvested stock option can't be exercised until the right to exercise it is triggered or vested, usually by the holder being in continuous employment for a certain period of time. Key employees are often granted stock options that vest over three to five years as long as the person is in continuous employment with the company. If the person terminates his employment and there are unvested stock options, the unvested portion of the stock option usually terminates and can't be exercised. *The company set up a reserve of approximately 10 percent of its outstanding stock for stock options to be granted to key employees over the next several years.*

SUPPLY-DEMAND CURVE – An economic graph showing that as price declines, demand increases while supply decreases. This same curve is also referred to as the price curve. *The company did not realize the supply-demand curve showed a huge increase in demand with only a small decrease in price.*

SWOT ANALYSIS – An analysis of the company's strengths, weaknesses, opportunities and threats. *The company performed a superficial SWOT analysis, showing the analysis in matrix form in its business plan.*

TARGET COMPANY – A company targeted by another company for acquisition. The target company becomes the seller. *The corporation was searching for a target company to acquire in a related industry.*

TERM SHEET – A summary of all of the material terms of an acquisition, negotiated between the buyer and seller before they enter into a binding agreement. The term sheet contain items such as price per share to be paid, liabilities that will be assumed or not assumed by the buyer, non-compete agreements for key executives of the target company, employment agreements for key executives and positions in the target company that will be eliminated after the acquisition. *The two CEOs met along with their lawyers and negotiated a term sheet for each of them to present to their boards of directors so the larger company could acquire the small company.*

UNIFORM COMMERCIAL CODE OR UCC – The provisions of state law governing sales transactions, securities transactions, security interests, etc. Almost all states have adopted a form of Uniform Commercial Code similar to the one recommended by a commission established by many states in an effort to create uniformity in these laws. *The company's founder didn't realize that when he ordered a new testing machine using a blank purchase order, the Uniform Commercial Code in his state governed the terms of the purchase.*

VENTURE CAPITAL – Capital to be invested in risky ventures that will not be liquid for a number of years. An example is when a venture capital firm invests $1 million in a start-up company by buying Series A Convertible Preferred Stock. The Series A Convertible Preferred Stock and the underlying common stock are not traded in the public market and, therefore, cannot be readily liquidated by the venture capital firm. *There is a large amount of venture capital in the United States, but most of it is being invested in very large transactions and not in small start-up companies.*

VENTURE CAPITALIST – Investors in risky ventures, such as start-ups or development-stage companies. Venture capital firms are usually limited partnerships or limited liability companies formed by investors with managers who make investment decisions on behalf of the funds. Venture capital firms are venture capitalists. In addition, wealthy individuals who make investments in early stage companies are often referred to as venture capitalists as well as angel investors. *The company approached several venture capitalists in its efforts to raise $2 million in equity capital.*

WHITE KNIGHT – A company that a target company goes to in order to be acquired to avoid a hostile takeover. *The company's CEO called the CEO of XYZ Corp. to be the white knight by acquiring the company on terms more favorable than the terms proposed in the hostile takeover attempt by ABC Corp.*

Appendix of Recommended Resources

Resources readers might find useful are listed below. All of these can be found on Amazon.com and other online booksellers.

Entrepreneurial Finance by Richard L. Smith and Janet Kiholm Smith

The Entrepreneurial Venture (The Practice of Management Series) by Howard H. Stevenson, Michael J. Roberts, Amar Bhide and William A. Sahlman (Editor)

Deal Terms: The Finer Points of Venture Capital Deal Structures, Valuations, Term Sheets, Stock Options and Getting Deals Done by Alex Wilmerding

Innovation and Entrepreneurship by Peter F. Drucker

Harvard Business Review on Entrepreneurship by Amar Bhide, William A. Sahlman and James Stancill

Thinking Like An Entrepreneur by Peter Hupalo

The Art of the Start: The Time-Tested, Battle-Hardened Guide for Anyone Starting Anything by Guy Kawasaki

The Directory Of Venture Capital & Private Equity Firms 2005: Domestic & International (Directory of Venture Capital and Private Equity Firms) by Richard Gottlieb (Editor)

Capital Vector's 2005 Venture Capital Directory (CD-ROM) by Capital Vector

Directory of Venture Capital (2nd Edition) by Kate Lister and Tom Harnish

Acknowledgments

Several people helped me with this book. Ginger, my wife, graciously gave me the time to work on this project and didn't complain when I spent many evenings in my home office editing and re-editing each chapter. Thank you, GG.

Diane Sears, through her company, DiVerse Media, edited the book and coordinated most of the publishing details. With her background as a former editor for *The Orlando Sentinel*, Diane brought a lot of wisdom to the process of writing this book. Thanks, Diane, for your hard work.

Rob Kaplan of Rob Kaplan Associates in Cortlandt Manor, New York, edited my early work and helped me focus this book on my intended audience. Thanks, Rob.

Diane Hoeksema, my former legal secretary, working on her own time, typed my dictation and all of the edited versions. Thanks, Diane.

Elaine Trench, my legal assistant, offered many suggestions and always caught errors I and everyone else overlooked. Thanks, Elaine.

Scott Adams, a talented video production artist and friend, produced the S-curve graph found in Chapter 15. Thanks, Scott.

Thanks to all of my clients who gave me the real-world experience reflected in this book.

Printed in the United States
By Bookmasters